D1201465

HOMAGE

NEW ORLEANS

A personal journey in search of the roots of rock and pop

Parade, New Orleans Jazz and Heritage Festival, 2009

"Follow your heart ... or you're fucked"

- Dr. John, May 2009

"It was when I realized I could make mistakes that I decided I was really on to something"

- Ornette Coleman, *Harmolodics Manifesto*

Photographs and Words by Leon Morris
Book design by Jessie Glass, glassfoundry llc
Published by Leon Morris, 148 Nicholson St, Fitzroy 3065 (Melbourne, Australia)
© Copyright Leon Morris 2015

www.leonmorris.net · www.homagethebook.com

Agency representation: Redferns/Getty and Hulton/Getty (www.gettyimages.com)
Marketing and Management: vera@twoshepsthatpass.com

National Library of Australia Cataloguing-in-Publication entry

Creator: Morris, Leon, 1957- author, photographer.

Title: Homage New Orleans :
               a personal journey in search of the roots of rock and pop / Leon Morris.

ISBN: 9780646938066 (hardback)

Subjects: Music--Louisiana--New Orleans--History and criticism.
               Jazz--Louisiana--New Orleans--History and criticism.
               Blues (Music)--Mississippi--Delta (Region)--History and criticism.
               Photography--History.
               New Orleans (La.)--Social life and customs.
               New Orleans (La.)--Pictorial works.

Dewey Number: 780.976335

Notting Hill Carnival, London 1982 – first prize, 1983 Greater London Council Photography Competition

I have been extremely fortunate to have a career (or more accurately a series of careers) that has permitted me privileged access to so many wonderful artists and performances over the past 30 years. If there is one key motivation for my commitment to this *Homage* project, it is to share the joy and pleasure, and the occasional transcendent moment, that this privileged access has provided me.

Music is a universal language. All peoples and cultures on this planet embrace music in one way or another, whether for recreation, pleasure, contemplation, solace, spiritual enlightenment, story-telling, inspiration, or movement and dance.

Despite this universality, however, the musicians responsible for creating and developing this rich tapestry of our collective cultural heritage are by and large not afforded due recognition. Indeed, many of the forms of music that I have come to love, and for which I am happy to evangelize, are essentially niche genres with very limited audiences. Ironically, the huge and lucrative audiences associated with mainstream recognition would not exist without these niche genres, because they provide the foundations on which the development of all popular Western music has been built.

Arthneice Jones, a blues musician from Clarksdale, Mississippi—the home of Delta blues—told me back in 1986 that "the blues had a baby and they called it rock 'n' roll." In the words of Robert Gordon, a writer and maker of films on Memphis music, rock 'n' roll is simply "the failed attempt of white people with a country background trying to play the blues". However you define it, there is something inherently accessible about rock and pop.

Rock 'n' roll owes its ubiquity and danceability to the backbeat, arguably first used in a hit record by drummer Earl Palmer in the 1949 Fats Domino hit, 'The Fat Man'. In 1956 (the year before my birth), Little Richard left Macon, Georgia to record at the now legendary New Orleans J&M studio run by Cosimo Matassa. Palmer backed Little Richard with what he described as a shuffle backbeat, a swing rhythm with accents on the off-beats. On the hit tune 'Lucille', Palmer responded to Little Richard's hard-hitting straight-ahead piano in straight time; the eighth notes are equal in length and the snare plays on the off-beats in 4/4 time. Rock 'n' roll was born—the Dixieland afterbeat had evolved into a rhythm that the world could dance to, and you didn't need to be able to swing to play it.

Eddie Bo, a New Orleans funk and R&B original, who died in early 2009, chose his musical career path in the 1950s because he recognized that people wanted to be entertained. He didn't think people could possibly understand all the intricacies and nuances of jazz music, but they could recognize a backbeat. Wynton Marsalis, probably the best known of an extraordinarily talented musical family from New Orleans, chose to preserve, develop and explore the traditions and lexicon of jazz, understanding that the backbeat has its place, but at the cost of restricting the conversation that other rhythms and musical forms make possible.

The complexities of jazz music can be intimidating to the uninitiated, and in this regard, I am particularly taken by my partner's description of an October 2009 concert in New York by young jazz saxophone colossus James Carter. I wanted her to hear the best of brave modern jazz in New York, and James Carter is as exciting and adventurous as any young player today. She likened the gig to going to a Shakespeare play: at first you haven't got a clue what is going on, but as you listen you slowly gain familiarity with the rhythm and the language, so you don't have to understand every detail but you can get the gist of what is being said.

It has taken me considerably longer than one gig to learn how little I know about the language of jazz, but what I do now know is that this language is rich and vibrant, capable of intricate subtleties and bold statements, contemplative moments and chaotic cadences. I am not a musician and have no natural aptitude for playing music; I have often thought this is the one skill for which I would choose to sacrifice any other skill I have developed over the years. It has taken me many years of discovery to learn to listen to the language of music, particularly jazz.

This journey can be extraordinarily fulfilling. Jazz is probably the only medium I know where the audience can genuinely and actively participate in the show, just by listening. This doesn't happen very often, but when it does it is scintillating and thrilling like no other artistic experience I have known. For a non-musician, those rare but precious moments when the interplay between musicians and audience is so intense and so real that the audience genuinely becomes a co-conspirator and co-contributor are exhilarating and sustaining.

My personal journey of discovery may have inevitably led me to New Orleans, but it began in the unlikely setting of Perth, Australia, where I lived until the age of about 20. Perth is the most geographically isolated city in the world—the nearest capital city, Adelaide is about 1,700 miles by road, and Sydney is another 900. Major centers of music such as London, New York and Paris all involved, in those days, flight times well in excess of 24 hours. Nowadays you can shave a few hours off flight times, but whichever way you look at it, it's the other side of the world

from just about anywhere.

Back in the late '70s and early '80s, when I was first exploring music as a young person's essential social and artistic medium, Perth was as culturally isolated from the rest of the world as it was geographically distant. The first time I became aware that there was anything out there other than pop and rock was when Sly and the Family Stone broke down the 'Walls of Jericho' on the local commercial radio stations with 'Family Affair' back in 1971 (I would have been 13 years old). It wasn't until many years later that I learned of the hidden parallel universe

Papa Lepke, Dread Broadcast Corporation, checks pirate radio reception on the roof of a north London housing estate, circa 1985 – one of a portfolio of 10 images, Kodak UK Young Photographer of the Year Award, 1989

of music history that formed the roots for the music I grew up on, chasing indie and new wave rock bands in the post-punk era of the late '70s and early '80s. Australia had a vibrant live music circuit at this time, primarily in inner city and suburban hotels. Interestingly enough, this period of late '70s and early '80s music has become pervasive in the Australian mainstream and continues as a mainstay of commercial radio airplay and Australian music culture today. But even then, and with minimal exposure to anything else, I intuitively knew that there was much, much more to learn and explore.

Escaping the cultural confines of Perth for the well-trodden traveler's path in south-east Asia, in 1981 I was fortunate enough to land in San Francisco, where I caught interesting gigs ranging from Frank Zappa to Oscar Peterson, Grace Jones to Bobby McFerrin, John Prine to New Order, U2 to Charlie Musselwhite. Pretty well anything that came into town caught my attention, and I began exploring my interest in both photojournalism and music photography. I picked up some useful magazine experience and joined a lowbrow photographer's cooperative with high-brow aspirations. Through this cooperative I met my very good friend Frank Dabba Smith, a fine photographer who taught me the importance of technique and helped me progress from a keen amateur to an emerging professional.

Arriving in London in the summer of 1982, I set up a series of darkrooms in unsavory locations as I struggled to survive in a tough town, literally opting for film over food on more than a few occasions. After befriending the bass player of an emerging dance band—my live picture of his band, the 'Impossible Dreamers', was only my second published picture in the UK music press—I fell in with a north London cooperative of peripatetic squatters with artistic intent of one sort or another. I remember going to gig after gig, heading back to one cold and damp temporary residence after another, processing film and printing 8x10 black-and-white prints in converted bathrooms, regularly having to add hot water to the developer and fix trays which would otherwise turn icy cold.

I also fell in with the 'Dread Broadcasting Corporation' (DBC) pirate radio station, attracted by their image, their ethos, their difference and their music. The world of reggae and calypso opened up through the annual Notting Hill Carnival, and a photograph I took at the 1982 carnival won a major London photographic prize in 1983. My new photographic purpose seemed defined when I was introduced to the people in that winning photograph by my friend at DBC, the one and only Papa Lepke—probably the best DJ on either side of the Atlantic not to get the success or recognition he deserved (although his sister, Rankin Miss P, went on to become a well known DJ on BBC's Radio One). This entree into the lives of first and second-generation West Indian migrants in west London became an ongoing project. I came to appreciate and share the intermingling of working and social lives lived on the street, all centered on the workings of a motor vehicle garage which acted as a kind of community center and focal point.

This body of work helped to make my name in London. Music was ever present. It was the soundtrack to the relationship I was building with my new friends in west London; a creative endeavor of many of my north London friends; and a sweaty outlet at late-night parties all over the city, where dancing to all hours of the morning was a badge of honor. Increasingly I frequented evening concerts and performances in the clubs and music venues that peppered London. In the words of Brinsley Ford, lead singer of the London-based reggae band Aswad: "Do you know what live and direct mean? It mean live and direct!"

By this time I was being regularly published by the *New Musical Express* (the *NME* had succumbed to me providing them with pictures whether they wanted them or not, and began to commission me to take live photographs and second-string portraits). I was also working for the weekly London what's-on magazines, *City Limits* and *Time Out*, and became a house photographer at the latter for several years. Many years later, I was contacted out of the blue by someone at Time Out to let me know my cover image from April 1989 of Oliver Lake on the Brooklyn promenade was being considered for merchandising as one of a selection of memorable covers from the *Time Out* archive. It hasn't yet come to anything, but it is gratifying to know that the image was being appreciated many years after Oliver was so generous in posing for the image at dawn!

I won some major prizes, toured my exhibitions throughout the UK and later Europe, and began working more regularly for the *Guardian* and *Observer* newspapers, before being recruited to the ranks of commercial and advertising photographers. Throughout this time I maintained my interest in music photography, although I had lost interest in photographing insolent post-punk wannabe rock stars, with whom I seemed to have been pigeonholed at the *NME*. I began working for *Black Echoes* magazine, which better reflected my new musical tastes and interests, and then hooked up with Redferns Music Library, the largest music library in Europe, which was purchased in 2009 by Getty Images. (Getty Images had previously

purchased the Hulton Archive, which holds my photojournalism collection.)

When I first drafted this introduction in 2009, David Redfern, the founder of the library, was very much a live and active presence in the music industry and in my life. David was always very generous in using his contacts and considerable reputation to open doors for me which would otherwise have been firmly shut. It was David who first introduced me to New Orleans, arranging introductions to the festival organizers, concert promoters and a range of key industry insiders and musicians. David and I worked differently. My journalistic background complemented his approach to stage and studio portraiture, and we always enjoyed each other's company. For twenty years we visited New Orleans together as friends and colleagues; New Orleans was our workplace and playground for two weeks each year.

I have been known to push the boundaries of good sense in the interest of an adventure or an experience, and David was a willing—if more cautious—partner in these adventures. He came to my rescue on at least one occasion, getting me out of a sleazy bar one evening on the outskirts of Clarksdale, Mississippi before the lunatic behind the bar could pull out what we assumed to be a gun. The payoff is that we have both experienced much more than we would if we had travelled solo.

David's death in September 2014, after three years fighting pancreatic cancer, rocked many of us in the small world of jazz and music photography. I was moved to write a long and heartfelt obituary that was published in the *British Journal of Photography* (www.bjp-online.com/2014/10/david-redfern-photographer-obituary/), with edited versions published in the USA and Australia. David's self-published book, *the unclosed eye*, convinced me that this Homage project was viable, and I strongly recommend all lovers of music and photography to check it out at **www.davidredfern.com.**

Writing about David, and thinking about the way he worked and the influence he had on subsequent generations of photographers, reminded me I had something to say about music photography which was as yet untold. The feedback I received from the current generation of photographers working under the Redferns 'brand' confirmed I was on the right track, and I take

Notting Hill Carnival, London 1982

up my reflections on the industry in more depth in a new afterword I have added to this book, 'From silver gelatin to pixels—some thoughts on photography in the 20th and 21st centuries'.

It is impossible to write about my career in music photography without reflecting on the changes in the industry since I began to take photographs back in the late '70s. I wish I could have been a better photographer at the beginning of my career, but nobody learns without making mistakes. I also wish I had been born twenty years earlier so I could have been around in the formative years of jazz, but that is something I certainly had no control over, and I am more than happy to doff my hat to the likes of Herman Leonard, William Gottlieb, William Claxton, David Redfern and Francis Wolff, who blazed a trail I can only hope to emulate. Nowadays I find myself one of the senior photographers in the pit. Most of the younger photographers on today's circuit never knew what it was to work with film and to not know what images you had captured until long after the gig was over.

As the idea for this book has evolved, it has also become increasingly apparent that the wider public's interest in photography has dramatically shifted over time. The afterword I have added addresses my thoughts (and frustrations) as a practitioner in this changing world.

In London, in the early part of the 1980s, I would shoot concerts for Redferns at night and on weekends, while my day job had graduated from photojournalism to the commercial world of advertising and annual reports. Lured by high fees—it is very hard not to be seduced by an extra "o" on what you would normally be earning—this new commercial world was temporarily lucrative, but ultimately soul-destroying. I was a hired hand, often nothing more than an overpaid technician. When the recession kicked in around 1993 and so-called blue-chip clients began reneging on payments, this short dalliance with the commercial and advertising world came to an end. I returned to Australia, disenchanted with photography, and unexpectedly carved out a new long-term career in Indigenous event production and then later in public policy. Photography became a part-time or occasional profession, with my interest in the medium and music photography sustained by the two weeks each year I would travel to New Orleans. I owe a debt of gratitude to the Jazz Fest production team, not just for being so generous over the years with their access and facilities, but most importantly for contributing to the economic engine room helping to keep the New Orleans musical traditions alive.

When I first embarked on the project of writing and editing *Homage*, I anticipated the process would involve changes and modifications as it unfolded. While the working title has continued to resonate—it sums up what I really want to say about the musicians who have given me so much enjoyment over the years—I jettisoned the original structure I had in mind for this book, which was loosely based on the concept of lost legends, living legends and likely legends. The inherent difficulty with lost and living legends is that too many artists are migrating from living to lost. Unfortunately, I have yet to see an artist migrate the other way.

Oliver Lake, Brooklyn Promenade, New York, 1989 (Time Out cover, New York Guide, London, April 12-19, 1989)

The trouble with moving to a genre-based classification, even one so loosely applied as in this book, is that there is no agreement on what constitutes different genres, nor do artists—shame on them!—behave in a way that neatly fits with genres. I therefore apologize in advance to anyone who disagrees with how I have structured this book; you are probably 110% correct. I also apologize for the exclusion of some artists I would have liked to include, but for a variety of reasons, did not. The most common reason is that I did not photograph the artist in question; I regret, for example, never photographing Bob Marley, Marvin Gaye, Louis Armstrong, Dizzy Gillespie, John Coltrane, Billie Holliday, Ella Fitzgerald or Oscar Peterson. I simply never had the opportunity or couldn't arrange photographic access.

If I have photographed an artist but not included them, it is only because I had to stop somewhere to avoid this project becoming ridiculously large. The judgement on which artists to profile was made on the basis of the quality of the image and whether I have anything to say or observe about the particular artist; in most cases this is more a reflection on me than it is on the artist. The judgement on which images to include in the edited selection at the end of each genre was made on the basis of design considerations in limited space.

I have also wrestled with how to include my thoughts on 'place'—specifically, of course, New Orleans and (to a lesser extent) the Mississippi Delta. New Orleans is a city I have come to cherish for all sorts of reasons, and my relationship with the city has spanned something like a decade either side of Katrina.

I have decided to publish some pieces pretty much as they were written at the time, because the observations are pertinent to that time and it is difficult to filter them with the benefit of hindsight. Additionally, I have included introductory comments on New Orleans culture and dispersed commentary throughout the book, as described through the window of a particular artist. My hope is that this will build something of an impression over time.

I have also struggled with how I might make the music available. If my primary interest is to share the experiences I have been fortunate to accumulate over the years, then the corollary is to provide guidance or opportunity for readers to see or hear the music for themselves. I originally toyed with the idea of a compilation CD, but decided against it on the basis that I am a photographer, not a record producer. During the gestation of this project, the increasing ease of accessibility to music on the internet has lessened any anxiety I may have had.

Of course, nothing beats "getting out there and catching some live local music"—the memorable catch cry for the live-wire calendar of the local community radio station and 'guardians of the groove', WWOZ. To see the music live, start by heading to New Orleans in the last weekend of April, first weekend of May (or for that matter, any weekend)—you can't go wrong.

Grace Jones, San Francisco, circa 1980

Thank You

This book is dedicated to the memory of the big man, David Redfern. The following people are also singled out for the help, assistance and support they have given me in one way or another over the years:

Sue, Ella and Marlena Jackson; Alpha, Dick and Geoff Pilpel; Dov and Gavin Morris; Vera, Amy and Michaela at Two Sheps That Pass; Jessie Glass, Matthew Goldman, David Foster, Bob Jones, Karen Celestan and Jazz Fest promotions; Betty Chouest, Stephen Hanneman and family; D Irwin Mackenroth and family; Lee Jeske and Wendi Royal; Michael Weintrob; David Guidry, Howard Mandel, Lee Grue, Kichea Burt, Jan Ramsey and Joseph Irrera, Frank Dabba Smith; Ebet Roberts; Carlos Sebastian; Nicolas Rothwell; Julian Ridgway; Ruth Garratt; David Hancock; Frances Green; Donna Bennett-Campi; Barry and Sylvia McCrae; Erik Brown and Adrian Day; Fred Miller; Hank O'Neil; Jim Megargee; Jason Knobloch; Mark Williams; Papa Lepke; Ronnie Briggs; Sabrina Grimwood; Paul Gates; Ginny Perkins; Eamonn McCabe; Linda Marshall; Pete Massingham; Wayne Tippetts; Lizzy Moore; Neil Spencer; Campbell Aitken; Ann Summers; Amanda Vincent; Michael Gallagher; Jim Cook; Bruce Finlayson AND everyone else who helped me along the way—you know who you are.

NEW ORLEANS

Spy Boy Waddie (Golden Hunters) with the Hot 8 Brass Band,
outside Tipitina's, "Instruments a Coming", New Orleans, 2003

NEW ORLEANS: AN INTRODUCTION

"No matter how far away from New Orleans I've gone and what I've done, sooner or later I always want to come back to my hometown for a roots recharge. In New Orleans, everything – food, music religion, even the way people talk and act – has deep, deep roots; and, like the tangled veins of cypress roots that meander this way and that in the swamp, everything in New Orleans is interrelated, wrapped around itself in ways that aren't always obvious. ... you can hear the New Orleans essence in the music ... if it came from New Orleans it has a flavour all of its own, a sound distinguished by the beat and, if the song has lyrics, by the attitude. In the music, its fonk, a syncopation on and around the beat. In the lyrics, it's a mixture of street smarts and soulfulness. If you want to know it , listen to Satchmo, Mahalia Jackson, the Meters, Irma Thomas, Allen Toussaint, or Earl King, to name a few. You'll find it with them, because they all got it."

- Dr. John, *Under A Hoodoo Moon* (Published by St Martins Griffin, New York)

New Orleans (or 'Nawlins' as locals call it) has always marched to a different beat, both literally and metaphorically. It is a city that either breaks the rules or reinvents rules that can later be broken.

I first visited New Orleans to photograph the 25th anniversary of the Jazz and Heritage Festival in 1994. Like so many friends and colleagues I see each year—every last weekend in April and first weekend in May—I return to what I refer to, tongue only very slightly in cheek, as my annual pilgrimage.

It is very difficult to describe to someone who hasn't spent time in New Orleans just how intoxicating this city can be. There is nowhere else like it on Earth, and it is to the eternal shame of the Bush administration that it did not recognize the national and international treasure it allowed to be devastated—live on the nightly news bulletins—by the inaction and incompetence that characterized the federal response to Hurricane Katrina. But for all that Katrina has done to fracture the social and cultural fabric of the city, there is too much investment in its soul over too many generations for New Orleans, as we eulogize it, to vanish and disappear.

What we have now is a new New Orleans; it can never be the same as before Katrina, but what was there before Katrina can never be denied. And what was there before Katrina was also a constantly moving set of cultural subsets and musical markers; inexorably changing and evolving as do any traditions and cultural values, however strong, however rooted in place or time.

This is a city that has embedded itself in the world's cultural sub-conscience. Largely unheralded, New Orleans has been responsible for the cultural alchemy (or gumbo) that gave birth to the two most important musical forms of the twentieth century: jazz and rock 'n' roll. This is not to say that the origins of both lie exclusively in New Orleans—that is not the case—but neither would have developed in the way they did without New Orleans.

It would, for example, be too long a bow (or too distorted a Stratocaster) to claim New Orleans as the sole or even the primary source of rock 'n' roll (Memphis may have something to say on the subject). However, rock 'n' roll and all its pop culture offshoots could not have developed without the backbeat, a New Orleans innovation to accent the off-beats, the 2 and 4 beats, in 4/4 time. This backbeat has become the underlying, all-pervasive and dominant rhythm of the last half century.

Jim Dickinson, a Memphis veteran of the rock 'n' roll era, who died just a couple of months before I commenced writing this book in late 2009, challenged me back in 1996 to "imagine the world without rock 'n' roll." That challenge could easily go further: to imagine a world without jazz, without rock 'n' roll and without New Orleans.

In May and June of 2007, in response to an uncertain post-Katrina New Orleans, I penned (or more accurately tapped out) a long piece that has not previously been published. On re-reading this piece, with the full intention of editing or re-writing it, I think it warrants being reproduced in full as an accurate testament to the city in the aftermath of Katrina. The review of the Neville Brothers concert in the following year picks up on the story a further 12 months down the road, and this is followed by reflections on the 2009 festival, particularly the Wynton Marsalis performance.

Additionally, I have profiled selected New Orleans artists, included the funeral of Earl King in 2003, and provided some more detailed descriptions of the extraordinary experience of street night life at either end of the French Quarter on one night in 2009. This cries out for inclusion as testament to the way in which this remarkable city can incorporate both new and old values.

The artists I have chosen to profile in the loosely organized sub-genres I adopted for this book were either photographed in New Orleans (usually at the Jazz Fest), have performed in New Orleans, have had an influence on the evolution of New Orleans musical culture, or have clearly been influenced by New Orleans musical culture in the way they work.

As for the contemporary story of the city, it is still evolving. As signposts on this journey towards renewal—still very much a work in progress—two events in 2010 stand out. First, on February 7th 2010, the Who Dat' Nation celebrated as no other city can. Against the odds (and the burden of history), the New Orleans Saints, 13-3 champions of the 2009 season of the National Football Conference, went on to defeat the Indianapolis Colts, 14-2 champions of the American Football Conference, to win their first Super Bowl. Was there ever, or could there ever be, a more cathartic or celebratory moment for an entire city?

Then in April that same year, news of BP's Deepwater Horizon oil spill in the Gulf of Mexico began to emerge. By the time of Jazz Fest, the acrid smell of oil was beginning to coat the backs of our throats as we partied in the French Quarter and the Faubourg Marigny. The unfolding horror of this disaster continued over 87 days, costing lives and livelihoods, and wreaking havoc on this uniquely vibrant and productive marine ecosystem. Foul oil contaminated the Louisiana, Mississippi, Florida and Alabama coastlines; the local fisheries, including staples of the southern food culture like oysters and shrimp, took a big hit; and the longer-term impacts on fish, birds, mammals and habitat, is still not yet fully understood.

Despite these trials, New Orleans has endured; it is, as at 2014, the 16th fastest growing city in the USA (out of 714 cities with populations over 50,000). Population levels are nudging up towards pre-Katrina population levels. The United States Census Bureau estimated that in 2013, the city had a population of 378,715—a 10% increase since 2010 and 78% of its 2000 population of 484,674. Over half of the 72 neighborhoods in New Orleans now have more than 90% of the pre-Katrina population. Growth is continuing, with the fastest rates of growth in recent years in those neighborhoods most affected by the floods.

In 2015, the city is alive and buzzing. At Jazz Fest, local musician and storyteller, Spencer Bohren, explains it is time to move on from his well-known songs about the impacts of Katrina. "New Orleans is back, if you haven't noticed," he proclaims from the blues stage. It is hard not to notice. There is a new life and energy to the city that shades the pre-Katrina years. For example, in Lakeview, the neighborhood I stay when I visit, real estate prices are rapidly rising and agents can't get properties to list. The previously dispiriting sight of empty and unkempt lots has disappeared under a wave of new construction.

New Orleans also has a significantly higher rate of entrepreneurship than the national average—as measured by the number of start-up businesses—and it is clear that the city is now attracting young people who recognize the opportunities the freedom and creativity of the city offers. Nowhere is this more pronounced than in the restaurant trade, where new and high quality establishments are opening up at an extraordinary rate all over town.

This is highly significant in this food-obsessed city. As one friend reminds me, there are two defining characteristics to the city: music and food. Local musicians will tell you that the hardest part of touring is missing the local cuisine. Many locals and visitors will invest at least as much effort in planning their dining experiences as they will their music program. Jazz Fest itself provides an extraordinary array of restaurant quality food ranging from jambalaya and gumbo through to oyster sacks, crawfish beignets and cochon de lait, soft shell crab, catfish and duck po' boys.

The current crop of younger lions of New Orleans musicians are growing up and entertaining the world. Second and third and fourth generations of famous and not-so-famous musical dynasties are building on their cultural heritage. The musical envelope that is so distinctively New Orleans is both the same, and as different and adventurous, as it always has been.

At home or abroad, whether the genre is jazz, brass, funk, hip hop or a new or hybrid music form we haven't ever heard before, there is a rhythmic and cultural sensibility that is uniquely New Orleans. It may not always be in the same way, or from the same parts of the city, but most assuredly, music and culture and creativity continues to bubble up from the ground.

Long may it continue.

Jambalaya Stand, 2015

Jazz Fest food, New Orleans Jazz and Heritage Festival, 2015

Watching the Sunday Parade pass by (just a few months before Super Bowl XLIV), New Orleans, October 2009

Parade, New Orleans Jazz and Heritage Festival, 2000

Frank Morgan on the banks of the Mississippi River, New Orleans, circa 1997

Terence Blanchard leads a horse-drawn parade from the Museum of Modern Art to the Jazz Fest grounds to celebrate International Jazz Day, New Orleans, 2015

Top Row From Left to Right:
First Three Photos: Parade celebrating 25 years of the New Orleans Jazz and Heritage Festival, 1994;   *Last Photo:* Parade, New Orleans Jazz and Heritage Festival, 1994

Bottom Left to Right: TBC brass band on parade in the French Quarter, New Orleans, 2014; Parade, New Orleans Jazz and Heritage Festival, 2005; Parade, New Orleans Jazz and Heritage Festival, 2008; TBC brass band on parade in the French Quarter, New Orleans, 2014;

Blues for Flood St – Ronald Jones, New Orleans, 2007

NEW ORLEANS
2007

Nineteen months after Hurricane Katrina precipitated the worst natural disaster in the history of the USA, the city of New Orleans can appear, on first impressions, to be remarkably unaffected by the impacts of the devastating flooding that deluged 80% of the city. My visit over two weekends in April and May in 2007 coincided with the 38th annual New Orleans Jazz and Heritage Festival. A veneer of normality was bolstered by as many as 250–350,000 interstate and overseas visitors making their annual pilgrimage to party in the birthplace of jazz.

It is quite possible to visit New Orleans and remain within the boundaries of what has become known by locals as the 'isle of denial'—the combined French Quarter and Garden District uptown areas that have always been those parts of town most frequented by visitors and which also happen, not coincidentally, to be the two areas least affected by the flood.

New Orleans is effectively a large and waterlocked basin. The French Quarter and Garden District nestle in an elbow of the Mississippi River, which marks the southern and western boundaries of the city and provides the moniker 'the crescent city'. To the north lies Lake Pontchartrain and to the east, the Gulf of Mexico. A simple rule of thumb is that the further you lived from the lake or the river, the more likely you were to flood, because the height of the land below sea level falls away from the water's edge. It is a very short but deliberate detour from the higher ground on the banks of the Mississippi River to the melancholy mix of wreckage and rebuilding that characterizes most suburban streets.

I first visited the New Orleans Jazz and Heritage Festival—or Jazz Fest as it is known locally—in 1994. I have returned each year since but two. I am not alone in this single-minded pursuit. I continue to meet people who share the same passion and commitment to the spirit and soul of 'Nawlins', and who continue to return year after year to play their small part in this two-week celebration of an inspiring musical heritage; a heritage that has, in one way or another, informed all of Western popular culture, but whose essence can only truly be experienced on home turf.

Back in 1994 I wrote, "New Orleans fosters a hybrid culture drawing on African, Caribbean and Cajun influences to create the hotbed from which virtually all contemporary popular music has originated. The home of jazz and Louisiana rhythm and blues is a party town: music, food and dancing is a way of life." A poet friend tells me "Culture bubbles up from the ground." Music is an integral part of everyone's life—it permeates all corners of the town and enriches the lives of locals and visitors alike.

New Orleans delivers to all tastes: trad jazz, modern jazz, improvised jazz, blues, Cajun, gospel, zydeco, R&B, rap, soul, funk, African, Latin, Caribbean, reggae and straight ahead rock 'n' roll. With over 600 concerts on 12 stages and literally hundreds of evening and late-night gigs in bars, concert halls and clubs all over town, Jazz Fest will inevitably showcase some of your all-time favorite artists, and lead to new discoveries of previously unknown artists to savor and cherish. It will also serve up some of the best and most memorable live gigs you are ever likely to see.

There is a rare phenomenon in live performance when the audience genuinely becomes integral to the concert; when the cliché of the crowd inspiring the musicians to greater heights becomes a shared and collective reality. Caught inside rhythm and melody, and wrapped in harmonies of sound and spirit, magical moments—or series of moments—ascend to soul inspiring heights.

The essence of great modern jazz is a conversation between the musicians. Time and space is critical. That which is not played is at least as important as that which is. In other words, great jazz incorporates virtuoso playing and virtuoso listening. Probably the greatest exponent of this art was the flawed genius of Miles Davis, whose spare and perfect trumpet has set the benchmarks for all that has followed. It is within this listening space that there is room for the audience to be the fourth, fifth or hundredth member of the band. It is also within this space that unforgettable memories are made and lifelong commitments to the culture are forged.

These moments happen in New Orleans more regularly than in any other town or city. It does so, in my opinion, because the town is birthplace and home, progenitor and muse. The sheer intensity of such a concentration of musical talent and musical history inspires creative excellence. If Jazz Fest was an athletics meet, more world records would be broken than at any other venue.

The annual pilgrimage to Jazz Fest has always been a major economic boost to the city, with the economic impact in any one year estimated at $US300 million. In the state of Louisiana, the cultural industries are second only to health care in the number of jobs provided for its citizens.

144,000 people made their living from music, art, film and food in the pre-Katrina world. But these industries, relying as they do on the bedrock of talent primarily resident in the poorer black neighborhoods, took a huge hit when the levees broke under the onslaught of an 18-foot storm surge rolling in from the Gulf of Mexico to the east.

Many of the musicians and standard bearers of New Orleans culture were forced to leave the city, others chose to leave, and those that remained endured the hardship of living amid the destruction. The local population was decimated, and with it the local market for regular gigs. Unsurprisingly, tourists were none too keen to visit a town with limited amenities and a reputation for unmitigated violence propagated by lazy and inaccurate media coverage in the immediate aftermath of Katrina.

Things are turning around, slowly—very slowly. As at March 2007, the number of people living in the New Orleans city area—255,137—headed past 50% of the pre-Katrina count for the first time. The Office of the Lieutenant Governor in Louisiana's Department of Culture, Recreation and Tourism now claims that two thirds of musicians have returned, 160 performing arts venues and 85% of art galleries have reopened, and 1,254 restaurants are open for business in the Orleans parish.

It is impossible, however, to escape the conclusion that many people are doing it tough. Every business in the French Quarter— remembering that this was one of the least affected areas—tells the same story: a tough time over the last 19 months, but Jazz Fest is making a difference.

Every individual has a story to tell, be it a Katrina nightmare, the trials and tribulations of daily life, battles with bureaucracy or small mercies as simple as the return of the mail service or the opening

Signs of renewal at Lake Pontchartrain, New Orleans, 2007

of a neighbourhood store. No-one has escaped the trauma of the flood. Some were certainly hit harder than others, and some were better equipped to respond than others, but all were affected in one way or another. In the faces of my old friends and new acquaintances, there is resignation and exhaustion born of the day-to-day struggle to survive, overlaid with the frustration of blatant bureaucratic bungling and dispiriting political opportunism.

It is hard to begin to imagine what it has been like for locals who stayed on, or those who returned, or are now returning. Rents, for example, went through the roof. People had no choice but to rent in the areas that were not flooded or were minimally damaged. These are likely to be the more expensive areas of town to start with, and their flood-free status immediately increased their real estate value by at least 40%. Throw in a dramatic hike in insurance costs, and rentals for many locals tripled overnight.

Homeowners had to find the rent for new housing while paying off loans and negotiating with recalcitrant government departments for assistance to rebuild their homes—and all this

time knowing full well that there was no guarantee any future investment would be flood protected the next time around. Throw into this mix uncertainty over the social and community infrastructure required to support a decision to invest time and money in rebuilding for your family's future, and the homeowner's dilemma begins to be understood. Why rebuild if your neighbors are not coming back and there is no guarantee of law and order, health services, power and gas, communications, schools or shops? Those that have stayed to rebuild their homes live in government-supplied trailers, reliant on local and primarily volunteer networks to provide support and build a community where government programs and assistance have palpably failed.

While approximately three quarters of the pre-Katrina residents have returned to the French Quarter and uptown areas, most of the neighbourhoods hit hardest by the flood are struggling to reach one third of their pre-Katrina population, and as much as 50–60% of that one third has moved back in the last nine months. Violent crime has flourished; police numbers are down and at least one station is still operating out of a trailer. One local told me, "Even native New Orleanians are terrified. We read the paper each morning to see how many more have died. I ain't never going to retire—I will be paying this off for the rest of my life."

Most of my New Orleans friends are stoic when it comes to the burden of small hardships: no local shops, poor mail and internet services, inability to find honest and fair tradesmen, pavements and roads being dug up again and again for yet another power, water or gas repair. Overlaid with these day-to-day frustrations are the systematic kicks in the gut from what can charitably be described as inept and cumbersome bureaucracy. There is a barely concealed and simmering anger directed at the inability of local, state or national authorities to take the necessary steps to turn this disaster around in the kind of swift and decisive manner that would be expected of a first-world nation.

Driving through the mixed wreckage and rebuilding of suburban streets provokes a contemplative mood. The traumatic events of August 2005 are close enough to feel like you might be disturbing ghosts. Most houses, even those being rebuilt or renovated, carry their official post-Katrina graffiti like a badge of honor. Large spray-painted crosses on doors, walls or eaves bear, in the quadrants created by the cross, the date of inspection (around ten days after Katrina made landfall), and code letters and numbers representing the origin of the inspection crew and the status of the house's occupants and animals: absent, dead or alive. Messages left scrawled on walls are eloquent testimonials: '1 dog trapped maybe more'—'Food Drop'— 'Normie Come Home'—'1 pitbull loose'—'Chicken under house'—'You loot you die'.

In a recent collection of post-Katrina writings published on a local website (NOLAfugees.com), there is a particularly poignant story of one street in the Bywater neighborhood to the east of the French Quarter where a dead body was found in a parked car. The car has gone but the parking space remains: "...no one parks in the spot where the body was found. This is, after all, a community of good people who prefer quiet natural death."

However surreal, and however disturbing this patina of memories, there are sights that beggar belief. I find two wrecked houses—one in the poor black neighbourhood of the Lower Ninth, and one in the middle-class neighborhood of Lakeview—that have remained completely untouched in the nineteen months since the disaster. In the Lower Ninth Ward, the gable roof of a decapitated house lies sprawling into the aptly named Flood Street. You can look in through what is left of the window below the roof, now sitting on the road. Inside are the scattered belongings of the former occupants, exactly as they were nineteen months previously. In the middle class suburb of Lakeview, there is a single-story house that has been lifted off its foundations and moved, at least 20–30 metres, to one side of the block. The front wall has been partially peeled back, as if to deliver a cross-section study of the kitchen and bedroom of the former residents. I am torn between voyeuristic fascination and disbelief that this can remain so.

On one of my visits to the damaged areas of town, I am accompanied by a local artist, Ronald Jones, who has, post-Katrina, lost his house and his marriage. In the last six months he has also contracted kidney disease and is now on dialysis treatment twice a week. He explains that while waiting in the seemingly endless queues for government assistance, people tell

Street scene, Lakeview, New Orleans, 2007

each other their stories. "The despair can take you down. At some point you have to make the decision to let go—let go of that ship because it is going down—you have to take your chances with the sharks because that ship will take you down."

The untold toll on this unique American city is that Katrina-related stress, frustration, anger and hopelessness may well have killed many more than the 1,570 people who lost their lives in the flood. One of my closest friends, for example, tells me, almost as an aside, that he attributes the death of his father to Katrina. "The pressure of returning to New Orleans was simply too much."

The ship metaphor used by Jones is well suited to a town surrounded by three bodies of water. New Orleans is basically a large basin, with the lip of the basin at the water's edge. As you head east, there is little or no protection from a storm surge because the coastal wetlands—a natural buffer—have been denuded over the course of many years by a 'development first' attitude that is increasingly being challenged by local lobby groups.

The historic French Quarter is the focal center for visitors. It houses many of the town's hotels, galleries, restaurants and music venues. Souvenir shops alternate with galleries and specialist clothing, antiques, jewellery and bric-a-brac stores. As you head away from the river for about four blocks, you reach the world-famous Bourbon Street—once a hotbed of live music, now a tawdry tourist drag selling sex, souvenirs and booze, afflicted by a permanent smell of beer and vomit. I read a piece in the local newspaper that reports a proposal to combat the smell by infusing the road sweepers with an artificial lemon fragrance.

There is an authentic and vibrant jazz strip to rival what Bourbon Street once stood for, but technically it is outside the French Quarter. The eastern end of the Quarter is delineated by the Esplanade, another of New Orleans' grander avenues—this one runs perpendicular to the river and if you follow its length for about 2-3 miles it will take you to the gates of the racecourse venue where Jazz Fest is held. It is also the street where the Neville Brothers' seminal Yellow Moon album was recorded in producer Daniel Lanois' house.

Back at its river end, cross the Esplanade at Decatur Street and you enter Frenchmen Street. In the space of about 300 yards past the local fire station there are at least eight different venues offering a range of entertainment from blues and reggae to smooth modern jazz. On weekends, Frenchmen turns into a street party. Music spills from windows and doorways, pavement buskers and barbecues ply their trade, and drinks are sold to passers-by from the windows of bars.

The opposite (western) boundary of the Quarter is marked by Canal Street, about fifteen blocks from the Esplanade and Frenchmen Street. The Quarter is linked to the opulent splendour and southern charm of the Garden District and uptown suburbs further west by long, tree-lined avenues: Magazine St, noted for its restaurants, cafes and boutique outlets, and St. Charles Avenue, a wide boulevard of stately mansions to which the umbilical cable cars have not yet returned. St. Charles Avenue trumpets the city's former glories at an approximate rate of 8 to 10 mansions per block for 60 or more blocks—a distance of approximately 5 miles. The area adjacent to the grassy slopes of the Mississippi River levee at the top of Saint Charles and Magazine has become known as the 'sliver by the river', which did not flood.

The comfortable appearance of prosperous normality in the French Quarter and Garden District belies the sense of frustration and struggle that characterizes other neighborhoods less endowed with southern architectural style, individual wealth and, most importantly, height. Jarrett Lofstead, one of the editors from the NOLAfugees.com compilation, explains one of the reasons for publishing in hard copy: "People should be reminded that things are not comfortable, and there is a tendency to cling to the delusions that there are signs of normalcy."

Canal Street, meantime, is etched into the world's subliminal memory as the street most filmed in the immediate aftermath of the storm. Canal Street links the Convention Center on the river with the Superdome, about 1.5 miles downtown. It was here that the world's media got it wrong on the myth of violence, but got it right when they shamed US authorities over their diabolically inadequate response to this home-soil disaster.

The inability to respond to the most basic of human needs in the immediate aftermath of the hurricane presaged the ongoing bureaucratic incompetence that has characterised and continues to characterize the rebuilding effort. In the space of the two weeks that I was in New Orleans, three key stories emerged in national and local media to underline the collective frustration of locals.

The first story was an investigative report by Associated Press revealing that "when the Army Corps of Engineers solicited bids for drainage pumps for New Orleans, it copied the specifications—typos and all—from the catalogue of the manufacturer that ultimately won the $32 million contract". The winning tender was from a company (MWI) that employed President Bush's brother in the 1980s and whose top officials are major contributors to the Republican Party. In May of 2006, prior to the start of the 2006 hurricane season, it was revealed that the newly installed MRI pumps were defective.

Next up, the Washington Post revealed that in the aftermath of Katrina, foreign aid offers from US allies to the tune of $854 million were turned away because the USA did not know how to process foreign aid. Offers of assistance rejected included cash, oil, medical teams, search and rescue teams, water, food and cruise ships for accommodation.

In my second week in town in 2007, a running story revealed worrying deficiencies and divisions over the Road Home program set up to help homeowners rebuild their homes. Not only had less than 20% of the $6 billion program been granted, but projections for future draw-down for the 120,000 applicants not yet serviced would leave the fund $2-3 billion short. The response from national and state politicians can best be described as unseemly bickering over which side is responsible for the shortfall.

The spat between federal and state politicians over financial responsibility for the relief effort is an open sore. A disproportionate amount of federal relief funds were directed to the state of Mississippi, also damaged by Hurricanes Katrina and Rita. Mississippi is a Republican state, Louisiana Democrat. New Orleans may well be the town of the trumpet—think of the legendary Louis Armstrong and contemporary exponents like Wynton Marsalis, Kermit Ruffins, Terrance Blanchard and Nicholas Payton—and the town may well be 'bent, not broken', as one bumper sticker defiantly proclaims; but if the cavalry are coming, it's not around this river bend.

In the sorry post-Katrina saga, there are several deserving villains. First and foremost, however, local people point the finger at the Army Engineer Corps who built the failed levee system. It is not hard to understand why. It was not the winds or rain of Hurricane Katrina that did for New Orleans—it was the breach of the levees as an 18 to 20-foot storm surge rolled in from the east and north.

I visited the section of the canal running perpendicular south from Lake Pontchartrain that was first breached—'ground zero' as it was described to me. The Corps is repairing the breach by pile-driving replacement pylons that appear to be the length of about one and a half buses. The pylons being replaced look about one and a half motor cars long. The older, shorter pylons have not been replaced in the rest of the canal. So there is a point at which the new, longer pylons directly abut the shorter pylons, which are proven failures.

Water moves to the point of least resistance, so locals understandably want to know, "what is going to prevent a breach in another section of the wall?" This became a presidential campaign issue when Democratic hopeful and former Senator John Edwards of North Carolina echoed the thoughts of many by saying that as far as he could see, "the Corps is just messing around with the levees. We've got to rebuild these levees. We've got to make New Orleans safe."

It follows from the studies of water movement before and after Katrina that the impacts of the flooding were both predictable and random. Higher ground spared, lower ground devastated, with anomalies everywhere. In the Lower Ninth Ward, the black neighbourhood in east New Orleans most comprehensively devastated by the breach of the industrial canal, something like 10% of houses were unaffected. In some streets it is possible to see flood lines as high as ten feet up the walls of houses on one side of the street, but perhaps as low as three or four feet on the other.

My expectation on returning to New Orleans in 2007 was that there would be a clear and defined racial context to the flood damage and rebuilding effort. I left New Orleans two weeks later distinctly uncomfortable with such a simplistic view and more than a little concerned that the long-term fallout of propagating this view—a double act sheeted home to the local (black)

Mayor Ray Nagin and the high-profile Reverend Jesse Jackson—is fundamentally unhelpful to rebuilding the social, cultural and economic fabric of the city.

This is not to say that Nagin and Jackson do not have a point; clearly they do. A survey by Professor John R. Logan at Brown University compared racial and socio-economic profiles of areas that were damaged by the flood against areas that were not. Almost all of the areas of town that were predominantly black (75–100% black according to the 2000 census) were damaged. According to Professor Logan, "If nobody returned to damaged areas of the town, New Orleans would lose 80% of its black population." In those areas of town that were damaged, 45.8% of residents were black and 45.7% of homes were occupied by renters. In those areas of town that were not damaged, only 26.4% were black and 30.9% were occupied by renters.

But this is just part of the picture, and a singular focus on the race angle tends to obscure the city-wide suffering and loss that Professor Logan's analysis also demonstrates. For example, 54.2% of areas damaged were white, and if nobody returned to the damaged areas of the town, New Orleans would lose 50% of its white population. Professor Logan also points out that "Closer inspection of neighborhoods within New Orleans shows that some affluent white neighborhoods were hard hit, while some poor minority neighborhoods were spared."

If you were unlucky enough to be a resident of Lakeview—a formerly proud and well-groomed middle-class (read: white) suburb to the south of Lake Pontchartrain, your house would have been, at best, inundated by flood waters of between four and ten feet. These rancid waters would have settled for three weeks in the ground floor of your one or two-story house, likely causing severe structural damage and definitely destroying all fixtures, furniture, white goods and personal belongings. At worst, your house would simply have been smashed as the wall of water swept away all in its path.

Lakeview is an area I know very well. For ten of the last twelve years I have stayed with the matriarch of a typically hospitable Cajun family in West End Boulevard, one of the main streets that parallels the breached 17th Street Canal. I like to think of myself as a quasi-member of the Chouest family for two weeks of each year, and I am known by a growing tribe of adult grandchildren and their friends as "the Australian photographer who rents my grandmom's pool house." The ground floor of the house was completely ruined, and the pool house or guest room I rent was also destroyed. The first thing I did after my plane landed at New Orleans' Louis Armstrong International Airport was to rent a car and drive straight to West End Boulevard. There were precious few landmarks to recognize and it took me two sweeps of the street to find the house I knew so well.

I am pleased to relate that Betty Chouest is one of the 35% of the former population of the area to be moving back to Lakeview. The house—and my pool room—have been completely renovated, and her move-in date is scheduled for a couple of weeks after Jazz Fest 2007. Her daughter has just purchased her a new piano—Betty teaches classical piano to a new generation of musicians—and I suspect her beloved old piano was one of the losses that hit hardest. All members of the family are excited to know I have returned, insisting that I have to stay in the newly renovated house next year. I can't quite explain the significance of this other than to suggest that it is somehow a symbol of returning normality, and locals clearly need symbols and traditions to hold on to in a world which has been turned upside down and holds so many uncertainties.

The saddest and most depressing images of Lakeview that linger in my mind are of formerly proud and manicured suburban streets now featuring more overgrown gardens and gutted houses for sale than houses being rebuilt. Lakeview is not a ghost town, like some parts of New Orleans, but there is melancholy and sadness in every street. But there is also hope, as people return and houses are rebuilt. As of March 2007 the local population stands at just over 9,000, slightly less than 40% of the pre-Katrina count. Locals can quote the numbers to you; when your future depends on your neighbors returning, every percentage point counts, and every small increase in numbers is a positive sign of rebirth.

What holds the city together is the spirit and passion of New Orleans residents committed to remain and rebuild notwithstanding the appearance of insurmountable risks and immovable obstacles. The glue that holds together this fragile web is the music, parades, social aid and pleasure clubs, Mardi Gras Indians, arts and cuisine of the region. In short, the culture and heritage celebrated at Jazz Fest.

As people wrestle their way to a fragile recovery, networks of friends, colleagues, self-help community groups and charitable foundations provide support and bolster the spirit. A growing network of supporters of New Orleans musicians and cultural practitioners has stepped in to fill the vacuum left by official inaction. Organisations like Sweet Home New Orleans (www.SweetHomeNewOrleans.org) collaborate with a range of service providers and

foundations to help "our tradition bearers secure stable, affordable housing", while the New Orleans Musicians Clinic (www. NewOrleansMusiciansClinic.org) aims to keep music alive—literally—by providing primary and preventative health services and outreach.

The most prominent and widely reported project is probably the musician's village being built by Habitat for Humanity (www.habitat-nola.org) in the Lower Ninth Ward. The program, conceived by musicians Harry Connick, Jr. and Branford Marsalis, will consist of seventy homes for displaced New Orleans musicians and a music center to be named after Ellis Marsalis (doyen of the Marsalis family, which includes sons Wynton and Branford as flag-bearers of the modern jazz movement). Sponsors, volunteers, community groups and future residents—each of whom must commit a minimum of 350 hours labour (or sweat equity) to the house building—began work in March 2006 with the first musicians moving in late last year (2008). This mission to "revitalise the music and cultural community within the neighbourhoods of new Orleans" is central to understanding the delicate cross-road at which New Orleans currently stands.

In one of those chance conversations that happen while waiting for a gig to start—this time while Lucinda Williams prepares to take the stage at the 2007 Jazz Fest—I get talking to a woman who turns out to be one of the earlier uptown locals to return home after Katrina. "What was the hardest thing about those early weeks?" I asked.

"The curfew," she replied.

"What curfew was that?"

"Two o'clock."

"In the afternoon?" I asked incredulously.

"No, two in the morning," she replied.

I couldn't help but laugh: "New Orleans must surely be the only city in the world where a two a.m. curfew would be considered a major hardship."

"You have to

Bar staff dancing at the Rock 'n' Bowl, New Orleans, 2007

understand," she said, "when we all got back together, we didn't want to lose each other again. We just wanted to stay together and we moved around as one big group, one big family—and we would see each other at all the same venues."

On the local community radio station (WWOZ) there is talk of the importance of music and food in the aftermath of Katrina. Up in the 'sliver by the river' there is a bohemian section servicing the students, the music fans and foodies. Walter 'Wolfman' Washington, one of New Orleans' most charismatic front-men, somehow managed to get hold of a generator. In a pitch-black street of dust and debris, the first post-Katrina gig at the Maple Leaf Bar salved the wounds, restored lost souls and worked its way into local legend.

Back at Jazz Fest, Lucinda Williams, a gifted Louisiana-born singer and songwriter, is pouring her heart out in what might well be the best concert she will ever perform. She tells the adoring audience that she locked herself in her touring bus for two days to prepare herself for this gig. "I went to high school in New Orleans in the '60s—this is one of the greatest cities in the world and I'm honored to perform here." At the conclusion of 'Everything Has Changed', her voice cracks: "That one really broke me up." Gillian Welch and Judith Owen join Norah Jones as the pick of the female singer-songwriters, while Joss Stone demonstrates maturity to match the hype surrounding this young English woman with a huge soul voice.

In the jazz tent, the saxophone is reigning supreme. James Carter and Pharoah Sanders bookend the new and old generations of modern masters. Cuban trumpet supremo Arturo Sandoval hits all the high notes while Roy Hargrove conducts his impeccable big band in a stylish mix of modern and classical. The Social Club of New Orleans fills the void left by the Neville Brothers, but Cyril Neville does not turn up as billed for this star-studded local line-up. The Neville Brothers are local icons, arguably spearheading the renaissance of New Orleans sounds in the mainstream for the last two decades. But they no longer live in New Orleans. Cyril, the younger and more outspoken of the four brothers, upset many in the post Katrina period by announcing he was heading off to live in Austin, Texas, on the back of public statements that New Orleans musicians do not get the treatment they deserve.

Allen Toussaint, a local producer, writer and performer of comparable iconic status, is the cultured gentleman of the New Orleans music scene. His response to Cyril embodies the prevailing view. "I understand why people leave and play in other places—we settle for a little less to live in New Orleans. But for me, I would accept millions less to get to live in New Orleans."

Sister Charmaine Neville and Aaron Neville's son Ivan are prominent at Jazz Fest and in gigs around town, but there is no sign of the Neville Brothers. This is a huge break with tradition in a festival dedicated to heritage; the Neville Brothers have closed the festival since well before I began visiting, and always sell out a run of three or four nights at the larger venues in town.

I last saw the Neville Brothers in concert in New Orleans in 2003, when they went back to their roots to perform at the legendary Tipitina's—basically a large beer hall which has hosted most of the best local music for the last twenty-five years. The Neville Brothers have, in recent years, been veering dangerously towards some of the soulless trappings of touring show bands. Tipitina's however, permits no such indulgences. The venue pays permanent homage to the roots of Louisiana music; a statue of Professor Longhair greets you as you enter the hall and his portrait hangs over the stage.

That concert was the best I have seen by the Nevilles for at least ten years. Brother Art, the elder Neville—also known as Poppa Funk for his seminal keyboard contributions to the New Orleans sound—had been ill for some time and needed the help of a walking stick to get on stage. He tells the frenzied crowd that he wants to buy himself "one of those amphibious vehicles—cause I'm telling you: we gotta be prepared". No one took him seriously.

Back at Jazz Fest, Harry Connick, Jr. gets the honor of closing the festival on the main stage. "As wonderful as this village is, and as wonderful as all the efforts are, we have a long way to go to bring our beloved city back." In the blues tent, two grandsons of Delta blues master R.L. Burnside have teamed with two white boys to form the Burnside Experience. This is not pretty, but it is compellingly intense: an awesome and powerful wall of sound straight out of contemporary Mississippi juke joints. Think Chuck Berry crossed with Sid Vicious, and consider that this might well be the future of the blues.

Night-time concerts around town feature many of the artists performing in Jazz Fest, and concerts and mini-festivals programmed to coincide with Jazz Fest. The Ponderosa Stomp, for example, is now in its 6th year. This year it is held on three stages in the House of Blues. It features a deliberately eclectic mix of artists—all of whom have cult status as "unsung heroes of blues, soul, rockabilly, swamp pop and New Orleans R&B". It is the brainchild of a local fez-wearing anesthetist—it is as if he has willed his vinyl collection to come to life.

George Clinton and P-Funk do not perform at Jazz Fest, but they do play at the Republic, one of the newly renovated music halls in the Warehouse district—a stone's throw from the infamous Convention Center. There is nothing quite like a P-Funk concert. Their primal funk rhythms are overlaid with weird and psychedelic personas drifting on and off stage—a dreadlocked guitarist dressed in nothing but a white towelling diaper, a dancer wearing what looks like a tassel lampshade.

Two years ago, four months before Katrina, P-Funk were my highlight of the 2005 Jazz Fest, performing at what was fast becoming my favorite local venue. The TwiRoPa, a converted twine and rope warehouse, had hosted some memorable concerts in recent years ranging from Cassandra Wilson to the Los Angeles Philharmonic Orchestra's daKAH Hip Hop Orchestra. Sadly, Katrina damaged it so severely it can never re-open.

A fifteen to twenty-minute drive uptown and Luther Kent—a former lead singer with Blood, Sweat and Tears—is doing two nights at a neighbourhood bar that would comfortably fit on a tennis court. Luther is a soulful cross between Joe Cocker and Barry White. He has sixteen musicians, including a nine-piece horn section, lined up down one wall of the bar. The sound is nothing short of sensational; these are some of New Orleans' finest session musicians and it is one of those rare privileges—to catch such an accomplished big band in such an intimate venue –that only New Orleans seems to be able to regularly conjure. Such are the joys of New Orleans; great and wonderful performances are happening all over town, in all sorts of venues. You know you are likely to be missing the best gig in town—because there are at least four or five 'best gigs in town' on any one night!

On one such night I reluctantly

Frenchmen Street, New Orleans, 1995

decide to leave a Pee Wee Ellis (James Brown's trombone player) concert because I also want to catch one of the rising stars of zydeco at the Rock 'n' Bowl. The Rock 'n' Bowl is a New Orleans institution unlike any other. It combines a ten-pin bowling alley with a music venue in one of the least salubrious locations in town. The floor area of the lanes is roughly equivalent to the floor area of the adjacent stage, dance floor and bar. It hosts some of the best blues and zydeco gigs in town, and Keith Frank's accordion has whipped up a party like no other I have known. A noticeably mixed crowd dances in the zydeco style, a kind of up-tempo folk waltz with partners spinning frenetically as if to match the lightning fingers of steel spoons on the metal washboards that distinguish the zydeco percussion sound. At one point I turn around to see the bar staff spontaneously dancing on the bar, one of them spinning hula hoops. As the post-Katrina slogan goes, 'Rock 'n' Bowl will never die'. Amen to that.

Back at Jazz Fest, in the gospel tent, Irma Thomas is respectful and restrained in her tribute to Mahalia Jackson. Dressed in white, this diva of New Orleans rhythm and blues pays homage to the role of the church as central to all African-American music traditions. The following day, Sherman Washington, the father of the gospel tent for the past thirty-five years and founder of the legendary Zion Harmonisers takes the stage. Sherman is an old and frail man still capable of preaching from his pulpit. The Gospel stage has been the scene of farewell concerts before—most notably when Johnny Adams, the great blues singer, delivered what was effectively his

own requiem in a spine-tingling duet with Aaron Neville, just four months before he died of cancer in 1998.

On Sunday, the last day of Jazz Fest, the day in which neighbourhood churches pulsate to the sound of church bands and mass choirs, we wake to the news that Alvin Batiste has died overnight. Alvin was the second pillar in the Marsalis family dynasty, a renowned clarinettist; this alone sets him apart among modern jazz players because the clarinet is most usually associated with traditional jazz. But he was much more than that—he was a respected educator and thus a revered symbol of the baton passing between generations. Among his illustrious alumni are the leading lights of the next generation of local musicians: Donald "Duck" Harrison, Henry Butler, Big Sam, Branford Marsalis and Harry Connick, Jr., to name a few. He was due to perform in the jazz tent that afternoon; Branford Marsalis and Harry Connick, Jr. pay homage instead. The closing act of the Festival jazz stage, is, fittingly, a second line parade in his honor.

The second line is the signature icon of New Orleans musical culture. Funeral processions begin as a sombre and mournful parade, then break into a wild and joyous celebration. The sousaphone (or oboe), bass and snare drum of the marching band set the beat while trombone, saxophone and trumpet swap rhythms and lead. Social aid and pleasure clubs—a riot of suits in bold and unlikely colors, feather boas and wild dance steps—build energy and spectacle while onlookers dance along waving white handkerchiefs (or whatever comes to hand) overhead. The more prepared twirl decorative umbrellas, while Mardi Gras Indians, in their brightly colored and intricately designed feathered and sequined head and body dresses, regularly join their African-American brothers and sisters to create an awesome spectacle.

The second line pays respect to the departed and celebrates life—particularly those unique elements of New Orleans culture to which the deceased contributed. Jazz Fest is, in my mind, one two-week long second line for the town of New Orleans. It captures all that is good about the city and provides locals and visitors an opportunity to share the pain and revel in the unique gifts this city has to offer. It reminds us all that there is nothing more important in life than sharing the good (and bad) times, partying with friends, celebrating our common humanity and working together for a better future.

The underlying and unarticulated fear—in what can only be a temporary celebration—is that another disaster might hit while New Orleans remains underprepared. If there was another hurricane anything like Katrina, then New Orleans would inevitably contract to the flood-free areas, cauterising the town from its cultural heartbeat in the poorer, primarily black suburbs. Culture would no longer bubble up from the ground, because the ground would no longer be lived in. It might only be when that happens that we will truly appreciate the significance of the current rebuilding effort, or more importantly the negligence of those with the power and resources to make a decisive difference. It is not by chance that the campaign badge of choice features the slogan: 'Make Levees Not War'.

Professor Logan concludes his 2006 report with the challenge, "Whose city will be rebuilt?" But for me, I chose to embrace the hope, humor and humility of the bumper stickers. In the bell of the trombone of the Storyville Stompers marching band, the sticker reads "renew Orleans". In the bell of the sousaphone of the Soul Rebels brass band, a black man embraces the Star of David: "New Orleans: Oy vay, what a city!"

NEW ORLEANS 2008
THE NEVILLE BROTHERS RE-NEW ORLEANS

**THE NEVILLE BROTHERS' HOMECOMING RETURN TO THE NEW ORLEANS JAZZ AND HERITAGE FESTIVAL
MAY 2008, 32 MONTHS AFTER HURRICANE KATRINA**

For two golden hours on the evening of the first Sunday in May, 2008, the Neville Brothers reclaimed their place as the musical torchbearers for the troubled city of New Orleans. Thirty-two months after Hurricane Katrina devastated the city, the Neville Brothers performed their first hometown concert to close out the 38th annual New Orleans Jazz and Heritage Festival, the USA's premiere musical festival, showcasing something like 500 acts on eleven stages, over seven days and two weekends.

From 1983 to 1995, prior to Katrina, the Neville Brothers closed the festival on the main stage, performing to the lion's share of the crowd, regularly in excess of 100,000 on the final Sunday. They have become New Orleans icons, their music and worldwide popularity coming to symbolise the heady mix of the elements that make New Orleans so unique: funk, R&B, jazz; a sprinkling of gospel and a liberal dose of Mardi Gras Indian street parades. Unlike other family dynasties representing the standard bearers of New Orleans' traditional and modern jazz—the slightly less famous Marsalis family and lesser known but equally important families like Andrews, Batiste, Jordan, Paulin and Payton—the Neville Brothers had not performed in their hometown since Hurricane Katrina. To compound the perceived slight to the hometown that helped make them famous, youngest brother Cyril—the most politically radical and outspoken of the four—was widely reported in the aftermath of Katrina as saying the city did not support its local musicians, declaring that he was happier living in Austin (Texas) and would not return to New Orleans until African-Americans achieved ownership in the local tourism industry.

Aaron did not return to New Orleans either, citing his asthma as a reason to avoid the toxins of a post-Katrina recovery. He is currently planning his return to his north shore home following the added tragedy of the death of his wife in 2007. This man-mountain—who could easily have inspired the Australian colloquialism, "built like a brick shithouse"—has the voice of an angel. Of the four brothers, he has had the most commercial success. His first single in 1967, 'Tell It Like It Is', charted at number 2 in the Billboard Top 100, and he reached the same milestone in 1989 with a Linda Ronstadt duet that revived his solo career and elevated his individual profile on the back of the mainstream success of the seminal 1987 Neville Brothers album, Yellow Moon.

Charles, the saxophonist, is widely regarded as the most spiritual of the Brothers. He continues to live in New York, returning to his hometown as a dual resident, much in the fashion of other New Orleans luminaries such as Doctor John.

Art, the elder brother, affectionately and descriptively known as Poppa Funk, has returned to live in his rebuilt house in New Orleans. Art is the creative engine behind the 'first family of funk', having pioneered the sound with his earlier band, the Meters (now the Funky Meters). "The Neville Brothers never left home," Art tells the largest crowd of the 2008 festival, as the band launches into an extraordinary two-hour set that celebrates their thirty-year anniversary and captures the upbeat mood of their home town's renewal. Not since the early days of their legendary uptown gigs at the local music hall, Tipitina's, have the Neville's demonstrated this level of energy and commitment, or produced such an intoxicating alchemy of sounds, rhythms and styles.

In 2008, joined by a stellar line-up of guests and band alumni ranging from Carlos Santana to Mardi Gras Indians and local heroes George Porter and Trombone Shorty, the Neville Brothers reclaimed the main stage at the Jazz Fest and their preeminent place in the pantheon of New Orleans music. Charles weaves his saxophone voodoo for the haunting bayou soundtrack, 'Yellow Moon'; then leaves the stage for a transcendent Aaron to launch into an incomparable version of 'Amazing Grace'. He had previously sung the same song to a privileged few in a packed gospel tent; here he lays bare the pain and humanity of all New Orleans, and sheds a tear for the memory of his wife.

New Orleans, in May 2008, has finally turned a corner in its efforts to rebuild and renew orleans (as the sticker and t-shirt of choice reads). Sometime in the

last 12 months, the mood of the city has turned from one of shock, despair, frustration and anger to one of possibility and hope, even confidence in some neighbourhoods.

Most visitors to New Orleans, before or after 'the storm'—as locals refer to Katrina—tend to stick to the major tourist precincts of the French Quarter or the Garden District. This is understandable: what tourists visit the suburbs in any major city? But these two areas are part of what is called the 'sliver by the river'—high ground that did not flood. They were then, and remain now, largely unaffected by the effects of the storm surge that followed Katrina, breaching the elaborate but woefully inadequate levee system and flooding 80% of the town. What has become clear in the renewal period following Katrina, and what was accurately predicted by those commentators angered by the shoddy and ineffective response of the authorities to the disaster, is that the capacity of the middle classes to come back and rebuild far outstrips that of residents of areas which were predominantly black and poor.

One of the first major breaches of the canal system took place at the 17th Street canal on the morning of 29 August 2005. The local newspaper, the Times Picayune, reported that the breach "sent a churning sea of water from Lake Pontchartrain coursing across Lakeview and into Mid-City, Carrollton, Gentilly, City Park and neighbourhoods farther south and east." The flooding devastated the predominately white middle-class suburb of Lakeview, sweeping houses off their foundations. Years later, flood lines remain on external walls—mostly just below first-floor roofline—marking the level at which the stinking and toxic waters settled.

Twelve months ago (in May 2007), only about a third of Lakeview residents had returned. The streets were blighted with damaged homes, unkempt gardens and ubiquitous trailers marking temporary residence while owners attempted to renovate their homes. By May of 2008, Lakeview has a new air of confidence and hope. Most houses have been renovated or rebuilt, and in many cases significantly improved over pre-Katrina days. The city's target of removing all trailers by June 2008 may be achievable in Lakeview.

Head east, however, to blue-collar Gentilly, and the picture is much more mixed. Head further east, to the predominantly black Lower Ninth Ward and then over the Industrial Canal into east New Orleans, and the picture remains bleak. Damaged houses and overgrown blocks of land (where wrecked houses have now been removed) dominate.

There are proud and valiant efforts to rebuild here. In one street a brightly painted yellow house is defiantly fenced off from its dilapidated neighbour. A musicians' village of identical houses with newly painted and individually decorated facades—the product of a mix of philanthropy and the vision of local jazz luminaries Harry Connick Junior and Branford Marsalis—is developing rapidly across two or three blocks in the Ninth Ward. The philanthropic efforts of Brad Pitt are said to be coming on line in the next twelve months.

In a town that gave birth to jazz, created its own brand of funk and developed the backbeat that made rock 'n' roll possible, the seismic shift caused by the devastation of Katrina and the consequent scattering of the standard bearers of New Orleans culture to various corners of the USA leaves an unanswered question hovering over the future of the city. Throughout the seven days of the festival marquee artists like Stevie Wonder, Cassandra Wilson and Bobby McFerrin pay heartfelt tribute to New Orleans, as do the many hundreds of local bands representing musical gems from blues, zydeco, gospel, Cajun, jazz, funk and rock genres. None, however, sparkled as brightly as the Neville Brothers. For two hours on Sunday, May 4, 2008, all was forgiven and all was forgotten. Festival Director Quint Davis closed the concert and the festival with a simple statement: "The Neville Brothers are the spirit and soul of New Orleans. The Neville Brothers have returned home. We are all coming home."

Top:
Aaron Neville,
New Orleans Jazz
and Heritage Festival,
2008

Bottom:
Neville Brothers
at Tipitina's, New
Orleans, 2003

Facing Page
From Top to Bottom:

Art Neville,
New Orleans Jazz
and Heritage Festival,
2009

Charles Neville,
New Orleans Jazz
and Heritage Festival,
circa 1994

Cyril Neville,
New Orleans Jazz
and Heritage Festival,
circa 1997

Left from Top to Bottom:

Mr. Green's caravan,
Lower Ninth Ward

Mr. Green's granddaughter next
to the caravan. Their new home
(in the same style as the house
to the right of the tree) is due
to be built next. The levy wall
for the Industrial Canal is in the
background. Lower Ninth Ward,
New Orleans, 2009

Musicians Village,
Ninth Ward, New Orleans, 2008

Right:
"valiant efforts to rebuild",
Lower Ninth Ward,
New Orleans, 2008

NEW ORLEANS: "NIGHT AND DAY" 2009

In April and May of 2009, at the fortieth anniversary of the New Orleans Jazz and Heritage Festival, the Jazz Fest program began charting its future trajectory towards major rocks acts dominating the headline billing. However, three things stand out as quintessentially New Orleans.

As if to underline the importance and interconnectedness of New Orleans jazz and culture, Donald Harrison, a jazz saxophone player of international standing, brought a Mardi Gras Indian rhythm section to the jazz tent on the opening day of the festival. Harrison is himself a Mardi Gras Indian, so this was no token gesture; rather, it spelt out the links between the rhythms of the street and the jazz idiom that evolved from those self-same streets. Then, on the same day, and on what is known as the Congo stage (traditionally reserved for soul, reggae and African acts), Wynton Marsalis, the international face of modern jazz, and Yacub Addy, founder of the acclaimed Odadaa! performance ensemble and a master drummer and composer rooted in the rhythmic traditions of Accra, Ghana, performed their two-hour composition Congo Square. This composition was commissioned in the aftermath of Hurricane Katrina and first performed in Congo Square in New Orleans on 23 April 2006.

Marsalis is something of a controversial figure in American music. He has been criticized as conservative and unadventurous in his championing of the traditions of jazz. I have never agreed. In this extraordinary composition and performance, Marsalis demonstrated that he has now taken a conscious step to redefine the jazz idiom, and he has done this through a sublime exercise in marrying African and American rhythmic traditions.

Marsalis, by his own account, has been undertaking a search for what he calls the "real American rhythm". He believes that the backbeat of rock 'n' roll—a New Orleans innovation—has placed too many restrictions on American music. It has locked the music of the United States in a perpetual cycle suited to dance, but unsuited to the more sophisticated story-telling that goes with African rhythms. Such a view may go a long way to explain why the largest crowds at the fortieth anniversary of Jazz Fest—well in excess of 100,000—came to see the likes of Bon Jovi and Joe Cocker, while Roy Haynes, an 83-year-old legend of jazz drumming, could only perform to an embarrassingly half-empty tent.

Marsalis' opening solo is as soulful and moving as anything I have ever heard; any doubts about his playing being too reverent or intellectual are comprehensively dispelled by the pain and anguish he conjures. At the same time, he maintains a muted hope that parallels the bowler-hat-shaped mute he uses to stretch and expand the notes. The composition itself is an epic two-hour journey that finds a comfortable marriage between the technique of a jazz orchestra and the rolling poly-rhythms of African storytellers. At its conclusion the orchestra marches offstage with the African musicians, the fading acoustic sound of drums and horns trailing off into a series of unanswered questions.

Then, as often seems to happen in New Orleans, the second Friday night of this fortieth anniversary festival throws up a series of extraordinary experiences that could not be anticipated or planned. This one night probably speaks more eloquently of New Orleans nightlife than anything else I could imagine or conjure.

I started this evening, as all good evenings in New Orleans should (or could) start, at a good friend's crawfish boil. Nothing could be more local than a crawfish boil and my friend does one of the best. A huge vat of water is heated over an outdoor flame. Into the vat goes a mix of Cajun herbs and spices, deer sausage, whole garlic, potatoes, corn and mushrooms. Then into this go the live crawfish. Many kilos of live, dark brown crawfish—a crustacean that looks like a miniature lobster, but is cultivated in the muddy fields of Louisiana (hence the nickname 'mud bugs'). After a few minutes the spicy brown liquid is drained and the crawfish—now red and perfectly cooked—are upended on long tables covered in newspaper, along with the cooked sausage and vegetables.

Standing around the tables, the crawfish eating ritual commences. Break off the head, and suck out the spicy juices (if you're game). Then squeeze the tip of the shell on the tail, and gently screw out the tail flesh. Crawfish are not large—the tail meat is

Frenchmen Street, New Orleans, 2009

rarely longer than a little finger—so repeat until sated. Intersperse with sausage, potato, garlic corn or mushroom (all infused with the unique spice mix) and wash down with cold beer and good conversation.

This crawfish ritual is the ideal starter to the offerings of a night out in the city. My friend and crawfish boil host has provided me with a late-night ticket to a concert at the House of Blues in the French Quarter, so I decide to swing by Frenchmen Street in the Faubourg Marigny on my way into town.

Bouncing on Bourbon Street, New Orleans, 2009

As described earlier, the glory era of Bourbon Street as the cultural engine room for New Orleans is long gone. Today, Bourbon Street can be described (charitably) as a tawdry tourist strip peddling a caricatured version of a jazz and blues illusion through a haze of alcohol consumption. Frenchmen Street, however, is the real deal. Changing and shifting character over the years, it is an aggregation of serious music venues, bars, restaurants and an organic street scene that creates its own night-time energy. Most Friday and Saturday nights, revellers take over the streets, turning Frenchmen into one irresistible and unstoppable street party.

On this balmy May night in 2009, and for the first time in my history on this street, two brass bands are vying for the crowds as they busk on opposite corners. The street comes alive as dancers move to the bass beat of the sousaphone and the unmistakable sound of a New Orleans trumpet or trombone-led horn section. This is much more exciting than battling and paying to enter the overcrowded venues, although no doubt they are jumping too.

Meanwhile, street vendors sell barbecue, Mexican and other tasty morsels. A coffee and cake stall sells the wickedest blueberry pies and chocolate brownies out of the back of a parked station wagon. I join the throng that is attracted to the brass bands, taking low light street-lit photographs made possible by the sensitivity of modern digital cameras.

It's time to move on—Frenchmen Street (at the eastern end of the French Quarter) will still be throbbing into the early hours if I still have the energy to return (or do not get diverted elsewhere in the city). A ten or fifteen-minute drive later, looping back to the other (west) side of the French Quarter via North Rampart (the street that delineates the northern boundary of the Quarter), I pass Donna's Bar and Grill—home of brass bands and trad jazz; then Louis Armstrong Park—site of the original Congo Square; and the Funky Butt—a music venue reviving an historic name but not yet settled on its musical offerings. Heading south on Iberville (one block shy of Canal, which marks the western boundary of the Quarter) towards the House of Blues on Decatur, which is one block from the river to the south, a car vacates a parking spot just before Bourbon Street and I gladly accept the offer. This night, I won't have to pay the exorbitant parking fee that can be extracted as the price for bringing a vehicle into the French Quarter.

It is now around midnight, and I have a short walk of about three blocks to the House of Blues. As I approach I see two lines. The main downstairs venue has a typically young crowd lining up for what the white kids in town call 'jam' music. Think of Jerry Garcia and the Grateful Dead, fast-forward twenty or thirty years and you'll get the idea. My line is altogether shorter, as I head upstairs to the smaller Parish room to see the Dynamites, a Washington-based dance band with a local New Orleanian guitarist leading an exceptionally tight and very danceable soul and funk groove. Charles Walker, a stalwart of the R&B era, joins the band onstage and the show is cooking. Charles gets draped with a feather boa by a member of the audience and I get the picture (in poor light), a minute or two before he discards the boa. Happy that I may already have the best picture I can get on this particular night, I decide it's time to retrieve my car and move it closer to the House of Blues, where parking will have eased up due to the late hour. That way I can catch the remainder of the show and make a quick getaway.

Walking back to Bourbon Street, probably by now around one in the morning, a unique ritual plays out before me—unannounced and unexpected. While the cultural axis of New Orleans music has shifted to the eastern end of the French Quarter at Frenchmen Street, back at the western end of the Quarter, on Bourbon Street, young African-American men and women are reclaiming the street. A string of cars motors into Bourbon Street, blocking it for about 50 yards and filling the night air with painfully loud music. These vehicles are basically mobile sound systems. An electronic display mounted in the car picks out the track being played through huge speakers that fill the trunk. I give up any chance of retrieving my car—it is the other side of this sound wall—and something is going on here that, for me, is new and strange territory.

This is bounce, a peculiarly New Orleans form of hip hop I have heard about but never seen or heard before. It is still a few years before bounce begins to get wider recognition as a major new music style. Young women are pumping their 'booty', sliding up and down car bonnets and over car roofs to one of the loudest and most insistent techno beats I have ever heard. This is not melodic and tuneful, nor does it sound like anything I have ever heard before. This is an aural attack of incessant hardcore beats. It is spine-tinglingly and ear-shatteringly intense. Young women match and better the fast and rudimentary techno beat as they 'bounce' their rear ends in the most blatantly suggestive moves. At one point one of the young women makes a point of smiling for my camera at her front end while she bounces away at her rear end. She clearly wants me to know that she is doing this of her own choice.

While there are a few women onlookers, the vast majority on the street is young African-American men, but surprisingly, there's very little sexual energy in the air. Some of the men seem disinterested, as if going through the motions of a scripted and predictable ritual. The energy levels do pick up from time to time as the women clamber on to the cars, pulsating their backsides to a feeding frenzy of mobile phones taking photographs—sometimes just a few centimetres from the object of display. As the men crowd around, more excited now, they take photos and throw dollar bills, presumably in appreciation. The women slide off the cars and back into the street.

In the documentary *Ya Heard Me*, the origins of bounce are explained for the uninitiated (like me). "It's not gangsta music, it's not R&B, it's project music ... it's truly a ghetto thing and if you don't understand, it is because that's not where you're from." I don't understand it and I don't understand how the young women can be so comfortably complicit with their street role as sex objects. This is hardcore softcore, right out there on the streets, and easily accessible for any passerby. It is puzzling and troubling. The images and behaviour seem designed to demean, but the street and the behaviour belongs to this new generation of urban African-Americans, and the street has become the theatre for this latest iteration of youths' ability to shock and disturb. I speak to a young black couple who are fellow observers of this spectacle. "This isn't the bounce we like," they tell me. "This is dirty or nasty bouncing. You can take your photos and tell everyone what you saw on Bourbon Street."

Charles Walker, Parish room at the House of Blues, New Orleans, 2009

Wynton Marsalis with Odadaa!,
New Orleans Jazz and Heritage Festival, 2009

Roy Haynes,
New Orleans Jazz and Heritage Festival, 2009

NEW ORLEANS ARTISTS

Allen Toussaint, New Orleans Jazz and Heritgae Festival, 2011

Clarence "Gatemouth" Brown, New Orleans Jazz and Heritage Festival, 2001

CLARENCE "GATEMOUTH" BROWN
18 April, 1924 – 10 September, 2005

Clarence 'Gatemouth' Brown, the 'Count Basie of the blues', was an institution on the Louisiana and Texas music scenes for over 50 years. Brown refused to be pigeonholed as a blues man, preferring to label himself an 'American musician'. He performed and recorded across a range of styles from blues and bluegrass to Cajun and zydeco, with notable excursions into jazz such as the 1997 'Gate Swings' big band album for Verve Records. The nickname 'Gatemouth' is said to have stuck after a high-school teacher likened his voice to being as wide as a gate. I've never quite understood what that means, but perhaps it says something about the family genes (or the vocabulary of the high-school instructor), because brother James, who also recorded in the '50s, was known as 'Widemouth'.

Brown's career fluctuated over the years. After a string of hits in the '50s with Peacock Records, he parted ways with that label and drifted into relative obscurity in the '60s. European touring kickstarted his revival in the '70s, culminating in a Grammy Award in 1982 for best traditional blues album, *Alright Again*, with Rounder Records. In the '90s he toured extensively throughout the USA and Europe with artists like Carlos Santana, Albert Collins, Buddy Guy and Eric Clapton, consolidating his reputation as one of the most versatile blues men on the national and international circuit.

In 2004, he was diagnosed with cancer and was also battling heart disease. He continued to tour, including a notable farewell appearance at the 2005 New Orleans Jazz and Heritage Festival. A little less steady on his feet than in previous years—he stayed seated throughout the set—he played his trademark guitar and fiddle with uncompromising spirit and feeling. I will always recall the way his eyes would gently wander across the crowd as he played, particularly as he peered out across his fiddle. It always seemed to me that this deep gaze carried with it an equal measure of warmth and curiosity; it was as if every live gig was, for Brown, an affirmation of his relationship with his fans.

That affirmation was confirmed a few days later on a rainy Monday evening when Brown was inducted into the Tipitina's Walk of Fame. He arrived with an oxygen bottle in tow, and was obliged to accept the honor with the oxygen feed lines strapped to his face. The photograph of Brown waving to the crowd, acknowledging the receipt of the award, is the last picture of him I took. The 'ghosting' in the image is only partly by intent. I had reverted to using the built-in, on-camera flash, because the makeshift tent set up to protect Brown from the rain effectively killed the outside lighting. I went for a long exposure, because when you get it right, the combination of flash and a long exposure can provide a much more atmospheric image than a photograph lit by the harsh light of a flash alone. On this occasion, the flash was way too strong—I'm not sure why; it just sometimes happens that way, particularly if you use automatic exposure settings—and the image is dramatically over-exposed. The digital reworking of the image, however, works for me; I'm not sure if it is because I was there and I remember the man and the moment, or whether this was one of those fortunate technical mishaps in which some of the best images are made.

Clarence 'Gatemouth' Brown died just a few months later. Hurricane Katrina probably hastened his passing, destroying his Slidell home and all his possessions on that fateful day of 29 August 2009. Brown was evacuated to Texas, suffered a major heart attack on 4 September 2005 and died six days later, at his brother's house in Orange, Texas.

Clarence "Gatemouth" Brown, New Orleans Jazz and Heritage Festival, 2005
Clarence "Gatemouth" Brown, induction into the Tipitina's Walk of Fame, New Orleans, 2005

DOC PAULIN

22 June, 1907 – 20 November, 2007

Ernest 'Doc' Paulin was synonymous with New Orleans traditional jazz. Born into a musical, Creole-speaking family in Wallace, Louisiana in 1907, Doc Paulin inherited the baton of brass band leadership from his uncle. Paulin formed his own band, the Doc Paulin Dixieland Jazz Band, in the 1920s, and remained a powerful, vibrant and lively influence on traditional New Orleans music right up until his retirement, at the age of 97, in 2004. He made traditional jazz his life work, and along the way played with greats like Kid Ory and Danny Barker. He also ensured that the tradition would endure by teaching and mentoring the next generation of performers, including his six sons (who now perform as the Paulin Brothers Brass Band) and other luminaries such as Dr. Michael White, Donald Harrison, Tuba Fats, Greg Stafford and Leroy Jones.

I saw Doc Paulin and his band play several times in the traditional tent at Jazz Fest; regulars know it as Economy Hall. There are some devotees who attend Jazz Fest just to stay all day in Economy Hall and luxuriate in the very best of traditional musicianship on display. This can also be one of the most uninhibited venues at the festival, because the intimacy of its size and the unabashed commitment to the music creates an unforgettable atmosphere. This is particularly so when a great band inspires dancing in the aisles and flamboyant parades featuring the twirling colors of second line costumes and umbrellas.

It was after one such concert in 1994, my first year at Jazz fest, that I asked Doc Paulin if I could take his portrait just after he had stepped offstage. Backstage at this venue is really just a small grassed area to the side of the stage, and it often feels like a family-friendly extension of the band onstage. Doc Paulin and his band had just 'raised the roof'; he and everyone else were milling around on a high. I quietly asked if I could take his portrait. He stepped aside from the throng to oblige, and gave me his attention for just two frames. The first was a straight-ahead portrait looking down the trumpet. And then he gave me the second image; a twinkle came into both eyes, wide open now, and playing up to the camera. His joyous expression summed up a lifetime of love for New Orleans jazz. I remember walking away with a spring in my step, willing the exposure to be right—it was a color transparency and it would be a day or two before I would know whether the image had worked as I had seen it through the viewfinder.

A year or two later the Barbican Centre in London chose this image for posters and related advertising for a New Orleans festival they were staging, and it remains one of my most popular images. I guess it is hard not to smile and feel good about life when you see that expression.

Doc Paulin's legacy lives on in every brass band you will hear in New Orleans. As his family says on their official website: "Our Dad was more than a musician. He was a great mentor to the aspiring neophyte."

Doc Paulin, New Orleans Jazz and Heritage Festival, 1994

DR. JOHN
Born 21 November, 1940

Mac Rebennack, better known as Dr. John, is a New Orleans original. He is a master songwriter, producer, arranger and piano player. He is both guardian and advocate of the unique New Orleans boogie-woogie funk-rock sound to which he has contributed what he calls 'the funknology'. His official website accurately describes him as "universally celebrated as the living embodiment of the rich musical heritage exclusive to New Orleans." Alongside Allen Toussaint, he is probably the most important contemporary musician, producer, composer and arranger of New Orleans music; he has been able to maintain this identity despite living most of the later part of his professional life in Los Angeles and New York.

Mac was born and grew up in New Orleans, where he was schooled in the traditions, styles and showmanship of New Orleans music clubs, Indian tribes and *gris gris* (New Orleans' unique brand of voodoo spiritualism). Survivor of a well-documented struggle with drug addiction and associated low-life events and run-ins with the law, he has always managed to place his individual stamp on the evolution of New Orleans music. In his (highly recommended) autobiography *Under A Hoodoo Moon*, Dr. John acknowledges his debt to Professor Longhair, "the guardian angel of the roots of New Orleans music... he defined a certain style of rhumba-boogie funk that was New Orleans R&B from the late 1940s all the way thorough to his death in 1980." Building on this legacy, the persona and alter-ego of Dr. John the Night Tripper was integral to the creation of what his website describes as a "unique blend of voodoo mysticism, funk, rhythm & blues, psychedelic rock and Creole roots", first concocted on record in the seminal 1967 album *Gris Gris*.

Dressed in voodoo charms and Mardi Gras Indian costumes (purchased

Dr. John, New Orleans Jazz and Heritage Festival, 2005

from New Orleans tribes such as the Wild Squatoolas and the Creole Wild West), Dr. John, the Night Tripper, adopted and adapted the old minstrel show techniques he learned in his childhood. "What I wanted was entertainment for the eyes and as well as the ears ... It was a kick to bring back that idea of showmanship to the rock and roll era."

Dr. John speaks with an unmistakable southern drawl. It carries with it a charismatic mix of street-smart cynicism and a full-bodied sense of humor that comes from some place only someone whose alter ego is the Night Tripper can inhabit. I remember eavesdropping on a late night conversation with Zigaboo Modeliste, a local funk drumming legend, outside the House of Blues in the French Quarter, where both musicians had played earlier as part of the Ponderosa Stomp. Mac's drawl can be so intoxicating and captivating that it almost relegates whatever he says to irrelevance. On this occasion, very early in the lead-up to the election of Barack Obama as U.S. President, he was railing against the corruption and ineptitude of Washington politics and what he and other musicians might be able to do about it.

There is always a frisson of excitement when Dr. John is around. Both the audience and the musicians react to the aura of his presence in anticipation and expectation of something exceptional and extraordinary.

During the Jazz Fest period, Dr. John might perform at multiple stages in the day, headline one or two sets per night, and then sit in on at least one or two other shows on the same night. He always makes it to the finale of the WWOZ Piano Night midweek in Jazz Fest, even picking up a guitar one year—an instrument he rarely plays since the ring finger of his left hand was shot off (and later reattached) on Christmas Eve, 1961 while rescuing a band member from a pistol-whipping by a motel owner in Jacksonville, Florida.

One of my most enthralling New Orleans musical memories was seeing Dr. John and Allen Toussaint playing a duet of 'Yes We Can Can' on facing grand pianos on the Piano Night dedicated to Toussaint in 2003. Just seeing these two legends together was thrilling enough, but nothing before or since has compared to the speed, skill and virtuosity of this particular duet. It was as if these two long-time collaborators were of one mind and one body, but four hands and two pianos; the notes cascaded in a symbiotic crescendo. It was impossible to tell who was playing what. Unforgettable—a musical moment that cries out for a recording if ever the opportunity arises again.

The only time I have seen Dr. John striding purposefully with a broad smile on his face, was in the second line parade for his old friend and kindred spirit, Earl King. Walking backwards, and fast (the local photographers have taken to calling themselves 'backsteppers'), I was on hand to press the shutter at the right moment; the resulting image is Dr. John as you don't normally see him. For me, this image also sums up so much about the spirit of New Orleans, a city that is dedicated to partying and celebrating life, even in times of death and sorrow.

Dr. John won Grammy Awards for Best Jazz Vocal Performance in 1989, Best Traditional Blues Album in 1992, Best Rock Instrumental Performance in 1996, Best Pop Collaboration in 2002, and Best Contemporary Blues Album in 2008. In 2004, he became the first American since the 1970s to win the prestigious French award the Académie Charles Cros 57ème Palmarès. His most successful recording, notwithstanding regular releases of originality and versatility, remains the 1973 album *In The Right Place*, which includes his signature tune 'Right Place Wrong Time' and a second chart hit, 'Such A Night'.

At an interview conducted on the heritage stage at the 2009 Jazz Fest, an innocuous question from a member of the audience—probably along the lines of what advice did he have for young musicians?—elicited my favorite quote of all time (to be read in the inimitable slow drawl of Dr. John): "You've got to follow your heart ... or you're fucked."

Dr. John (with Lucy Barnett, Ricky Castrillo and Geraldine Wyckoff) at Earl King Funeral Procession, New Orleans, 2003

Dr. John at
re-opening of Carver
Theatre in Treme,
New Orleans, 2014

Dr. John and Zigaboo
Modeliste outside the
House of Blues,
New Orleans, 2008

EARL KING
7 February, 1934 – 17 April, 2003

Born Earl Silas Johnson IV, Earl King is acknowledged in his home town as one of the most significant musicians in the development of New Orleans R&B music, but he is another of those Louisiana artists who never reaped the financial rewards or national and international acclaim he deserved. Consequently, when he died just one week prior to the New Orleans Jazz and Heritage Festival of 2003, there was a question mark over whether the funeral parade he warranted would take place.

A New Orleans jazz funeral is like no other. It is a right royal send-off and King's befitted both his surname and his status as the "the reigning monarch of New Orleans rhythm and blues". (http://www.blues. co.nz/news/article.php?id=273)

King composed some New Orleans standards including 'Come On' (popularized by Jimi Hendrix), 'Big Chief' (the seminal New Orleans street party song played most memorably by Professor Longhair), and 'Trick Bag' (covered by Robert Palmer among others and also picked up by Luther Kent as the name for his incomparably tight local blues big band). One of his greatest admirers and sometime former collaborator is the redoubtable Dr. John, who was one of many local luminaries—including Dave Bartholomew, Deacon John, Aaron and Art Neville, Irma Thomas, Charlie Miller, Willie Tee, Henry Butler and Eddie Bo—to perform a musical tribute at his wake on 13 April 2003.

I arrived early at the stately Gallier Hall on St. Charles Avenue where King lay, waiting to be given his send-off. Uncomfortable being an outsider at an insider's event, I left the tributes and casket walk-by to his friends, and waited outside with the patient crowd for the traditional jazz second line procession which had been advertised would follow the service. King's coffin was taken, in sombre mood, from the Hall to a horse-drawn carriage. For another five or ten minutes, the procession proceeded in sadness and reflection. Then, at the call of the trumpet, the parade transformed to a joyous celebration of his life.

Wanda Rouzan was partying up such a storm, on what was a typically hot and humid New Orleans day, that I learned later that evening (at a reflective dinner party with local musicians and festival staff) that she had collapsed with heat exhaustion and been taken to hospital. J. Monque'D, a notable local musician and character around town, shed a public tear as the parade finished and the hearse departed for a private family burial. Earlier, during this second line parade, I caught Dr. John in an uncharacteristically upbeat pose. He was positively bouncing along the street, walking stick in hand, a broad and open smile across his face. I have never seen Dr. John in comparable mood before or since—as fitting a tribute as I can think of for his good friend, the great Earl King.

Earl King funeral: leaving Gallier Hall, New Orleans, 2008

Earl King, New Orleans Jazz and Heritage Festival, 1998

Earl King funeral: sombre beginning of procession,
New Orleans, 2008

EDWIN JOSEPH BOCAGE ('EDDIE BO')
20 September, 1930 – 18 March, 2009

Eddie Bo was a flamboyant, prolific and much-loved New Orleans keyboard player, songwriter and producer/arranger who died in early 2009, shortly after the death of his occasional playing partner Snooks Eaglin. The loss of Eaglin and Bo left a gaping hole in the heritage part of the 2009 New Orleans Jazz and Heritage Festival. Bo was an exceptionally talented pianist, a great showman, a fine songwriter and a much-admired producer. I will always remember him as the party master of New Orleans, a role he played with gusto at the annual WWOZ Piano Night on the Monday night after the first weekend of each Jazz Festival.

Piano Night has become a New Orleans institution, and Bo was a driving force behind its success. The very best of New Orleans' session musicians back a host of piano and keyboard players from early afternoon through to the early hours of the morning. Each Piano Night is dedicated to one artist, and Bo was honored in 2001, 2002 and posthumously in 2009.

I would always tune in to the live radio broadcast on and off throughout the day—I like

piano but not twelve hours straight!—and then make my way to the star-studded finale. Usually the night culminates in the likes of Allen Toussaint, Dr. John, Davell Crawford, and Marcia Ball taking the stage together, trading piano licks across facing grand pianos, with electric or Hammond organs positioned at the rear or side stage. At the center of all this organized mayhem was none other than Eddie Bo, building the groove, holding the show together, and whipping both the musicians and the crowd into a frenzy.

Bo had made the decision early in his music career to dedicate himself to the groove. He aimed to entertain and always performed in style. He dressed well, lit up the stage with his broad and genuine smile, and he knew how to part-ay.

Eddie Bo grew up in the Algiers and Ninth Ward sections of New Orleans and hailed from a family of Creole musicians with impressive jazz pedigrees. After his release from the U.S. army (where he was given the nickname Spider because of his skills in the boxing ring), Bo chose

R&B for his musical path. Bo believed most audiences couldn't understand the intricacies of jazz and just wanted to be entertained: "They understood what a backbeat was; they could feel the rhythm."

He started recording in 1995 with Ace Records and went on to work with more than forty different record labels. He is second only to the legendary Fats Domino for the number of singles released by a New Orleans artist. Unlike Fats Domino, however, he was never rewarded with the national hits he probably deserved. His second release, 'I'm Wise', in 1956, was later recorded by Little Richard as the hit single 'Slippin' and Slidin', and Bo also had early success with 'My Dearest Darling' written for Etta James and 'In the Same Old Way' for Tommy Ridgley.

Bo's most popular release in his own right was probably the 1971 hit, 'Check Your Bucket'. This record underscored Bo's significance as one of the founders of the emerging New Orleans funk sound, along with artists like Willie Tee and the Meters. Bo later opened a cafe called Check Your Bucket, which was subsequently destroyed by Hurricane Katrina.

Eddie Bo could not only write the song, play the groove and sing the tune, he could also 'get on down'. Two of my favorite New Orleans images come from the 2003 Piano Night where Eddie Bo and long-time sideman Herb Hardesty proved you are never too old to dance dirty.

Left: Eddie Bo, New Orleans Jazz and Heritage Festival, 2003
Right: Eddie Bo, WWOZ Piano Night, New Orleans, 2003

FATS DOMINO
Born 26 February, 1928

Antoine 'Fats' Domino Jr. is a unique New Orleans artistic treasure. He was a pioneer of early rock 'n' roll and second only to Elvis Presley for the number of hit records from that era. *Rolling Stone* magazine ranked him 25th in their 100 greatest artists of all time, and he was an inaugural inductee in the Rock and Roll Hall of Fame in 1986. He was awarded a Grammy Lifetime Achievement Award in 1987 and a National Medal of the Arts in 1998.

Born to a French Creole family, he was a permanent fixture in the Lower Ninth Ward until he was rescued from his flooded home during the confused aftermath of Hurricane Katrina. This was, however, not before news wires around the world had flashed his demise following the release of a photograph of his house painted with the message, "RIP Fats. You will be missed".

Back in the 1980s, Domino had decided there was no reason to leave New Orleans. His back-catalogue of hits from the 50s and 60s provided a regular stream of royalties and he didn't enjoy touring. In common with many other locals, he thought hometown food could not be replicated or bettered anywhere else in the world. (Fats himself is said to be a fine cook, with a specialty dish of rice and beans.) So, why leave?

Photographing Fats Domino is always exciting because he rarely plays (just a few outings over the last twenty years at Jazz Fest) and he is music royalty. Seeing Fats Domino play is like going back to the birth of rock 'n' roll; his first big hit, the 1949 recording, 'The Fat Man', features Domino's vocals and piano over an Earl Palmer backbeat. And you never know just who will be in his band, because he can draw on the best collaborators and sidemen in town; imagine, for example, a brass section that includes Dave Bartholomew, Herb Hardesty, Alvin 'Red' Tyler and Reggie Houston!

You have to be on your toes to photograph a piano player, because when the artist is seated a there is usually only a very narrow angle from which to get the best shot. And you also have to be ready for Fats to rise from the piano stool and push the piano across the stage while playing and singing—it's a remarkable feat and his trademark, but not so easy an image to capture or do justice to in a crowded pit.

His best known songs include 'Ain't That a Shame', 'Blueberry Hill' and 'I'm Walkin'', which was a number one R&B hit for six weeks in 1957 (the year of my birth), before crossing over to reach number four in the pop charts. Through the passage of time, the lyrics took on added (and originally unintended) poignancy during the aftermath of Katrina: "I'm hopin' that you'll come back to me."

Left: Fats Domino, New Orleans Jazz and Heritage Festival, 2001
Below: Fats Domino, Gala Dinner, New Orleans Jazz and Heritage Festival, 2002

GLEN DAVID ANDREWS

Born 27 April, 1980

Glen David Andrews grew up in Treme, and draws on a uniquely New Orleans musical education that was one part gospel church music and one part second line parade. His grandfather was Jessie Hill, he called Lionel Batiste 'uncle', and he would run into Ernie K-Doe in the neighborhood. Andrews' website tells the following story: "According to family folklore, Anthony 'Tuba Fats' Lacen, a patriarch of modern New Orleans music, directed the bell of his horn toward Andrews's mother's belly as a way to induce labor. Andrews was born the following day."

The most famous of Glen David's generation of cousins in the extraordinary Andrews family is the precociously talented Trombone Shorty (Troy Andrews). The story goes that Troy told Glen that he had to learn to sing and become a frontman, because Troy preferred playing the trombone to being the frontman. Now both Glen and Troy have become consummate performers and band leaders, Troy plays trumpet more than trombone, and Glen tends to use his trombone more as a stage prop than a musical instrument (although he still knows how to blow if the mood takes his fancy).

In October 2009, I went to catch Glen at one of his typically small but energetic performances at Antoine's Restaurant in the French Quarter. Over a drink at the bar, I asked if he could help me find the second line parade that coming weekend. The 'Prince of Treme' took it upon himself to ensure that I would see for myself the proud street culture from which

Glen David Andrews, birthday concert at dba club, Frenchmen Street, New Orleans, 2009

Andrews' roots and music derived.

2009 was in many ways a breakout year for Glen David. His emerging reputation for explosive and spellbinding live performances had stamped him as a star of rare talent and unbridled energy. In May of that year, John Pareles of the *New York Times* reviewed his gospel tent performance as "a sequined star turn for the Lord: showy, unpredictable, head-turning and ecstatic". The same paper used a photograph of Andrews performing in the gospel tent to illustrate their review of the fortieth anniversary of Jazz Fest. That review was titled 'From Shaky Start to Enduring Tradition', and in retrospect, might yet come to describe the career of Glen David Andrews.

The thing about a Glen David Andrews gig in this period was that it didn't matter if there were three people in the audience or three thousand. Glen would give it his all and play to each and every person with the zeal of a missionary. His performances were always highly charged theatrical and musical tour de forces. It was as if Louis Armstrong had swapped trumpet for trombone, got high on an erratic cocktail of alcohol and drugs, and by force of will bent his considerable musical talent to winning the hearts, minds, hips and feet of whatever audience he was inducting that evening.

Against a backdrop of personal tragedy—for example, his cousin Darnell 'D-Boy' Andrews was murdered in the streets of New Orleans—Glen David has always spoken out strongly for the right to parade in the streets of the city. In October 2007, he and his brother, snare drummer Derrick Tabb, were arrested for leading a second line through Treme to commemorate the death of New Birth Brass Band tuba player Kerwin James. In the popular HBO TV series, *Treme*, which has exposed New Orleans culture to the world, Andrews was chosen to lead the anti-violence second line parade. In filmmaker Spike Lee's 2006 Katrina documentary, *When the Levees Broke*, Andrews led the mock funeral procession in which he changes the words in the last line of the funeral hymn 'I'll Fly Away' to 'New Orleans will never go away'. In 2007, in the very real streets of Treme, it was this hymn that the musicians were singing when Andrews and Tabb was arrested.

Fast forward a few years to 2014, and all the talk is about *Redemption*, a more reflective and nuanced album released after a lengthy and very public rehabilitation from alcohol and drug addiction, which followed a 2012 felony conviction for domestic violence. Andrews is still performing at high energy, and still knows how to work a crowd, but there is something approaching evangelical zeal in the way he sells his new, cleaner, lifestyle and the way in which he draws on his friends and family for musical inspiration and personal support.

Andrews has described his popular brass band anthem, 'Knock with Me, Rock with Me', as a rallying cry: "Let's get together and do what we got to do." Only time will answer the prophetic question he asks in the same song: "Ten years from now, where will I be? Will I be shining like a star, bright as the eye can see? Or will I be kicking the breeze hanging on St. Philip Street?"

HENRY BUTLER
Born 21 September, 1949

Henry Butler is quintessentially New Orleans. A phenomenally gifted piano player, singer and composer, he is equally adept in modern jazz, foot stomping barrel-house blues, and all genres and unexpected tangents in between. A self-described ambassador for the inspirational and uplifting role of New Orleans music, particularly in the wake of Hurricane Katrina, which destroyed his home in the neighbourhood of Gentilly, he is a perennial favorite with local musicians and fans alike.

Henry Butler is one of those artists that can headline or guest on as many as three or four gigs on the same night. He not only seems to have boundless energy to attack his piano with lightning speed and percussive bravado, he has an encyclopedic knowledge of the full lexicon of modern American music, and he brings this with him to every gig; from a straight-ahead three-piece jazz combo through to a Delta deep blues session, or a funky New Orleans R&B style jam in which the influence and legacy of the legendary Professor Longhair lives alongside the chants and rhythms of Mardi Gras Indians.

When I think of Henry Butler, four things come to mind. First, I have never regretted going to a Henry Butler performance or a gig where he is sitting in. His piano playing is breathtakingly powerful and engaging, whatever style he is playing. Second, I have never found a recording that does justice to the skill, passion and commitment to entertain and inspire that he brings to every live performance, but has yet to capture in the studio. Third, I have never understood why he is not as respected and loved outside of New Orleans as he is on home turf. And fourth, I will be forever grateful for one of the most moving and powerful musical experiences in my life at a poorly attended gig back in 1995.

At this gig, upstairs in the newly opened Funky Butt club, Henry was playing in a three-piece jazz combination, which was his primary recording vehicle in his earlier years. He was mining his back catalogue, which these days can only be sourced from specialist second-hand record stores, and he launched into an extended version of 'Music Came', an extraordinary and wonderful composition he had recorded for MCA Impulse in 1987, and which was written by his mentor, the late lamented jazz musician and educator, Alvin Batiste. In the manner of all great jazz playing, the trio meandered on and off the recurring theme and motif of this lyrical, melodic and rhythmically driven piece. Henry led the way, tracing the roots of African-American music through slavery, gospel, blues and jazz to rock 'n' roll. This was more than just a stunning tour de force of musical beauty; it was a deep and heartfelt exploration of the link between the African-American condition and the history of contemporary music in America.

"Way down deep from the depths of sorrow, music came.
Now I stake my claim, claim to be free
Because I know what it means to have true identity,
Because music came."

Top to Bottom:

Henry Butler, New Orleans Jazz and Heritage Festival, 2003

Henry Butler, Saenger Theatre, New Orleans, 2003

Henry Butler, New Orleans Jazz and Heritage Festival, 2014

Henry Butler and Big Chief Monk Boudreaux,
Sweet Home New Orleans benefit concert,
New Orleans, 2007

IRMA THOMAS
Born 18 February, 1941

Louisiana-born Irma Thomas is the 'Soul Queen of New Orleans'. She is probably the most accomplished artist of her generation not to have achieved the kind of success enjoyed by contemporaries such as Aretha Franklin, Dionne Warwick, Patti LaBelle and Etta James. Rounder Records, with whom she has been recording for 25 years after short-lived associations with Minit, Imperial, Chess Canon, Atlantic and RCS, describe her as "one of America's most distinctive and classic singers, a treasure from the golden age of soul music who remains as compelling and powerful as ever." Possibly best known for her 1960s hits such as 'Time Is On My Side', 'It's Raining' and 'Wish Someone Would Care', she had to wait until 2006 to win her first Grammy Award: Best Contemporary Blues Album for After the Rain. Her most recent release celebrates fifty years in the industry.

Irma Thomas is a perennial favorite at the New Orleans Jazz and Heritage Festival. Jazz Fest without Irma is as unthinkable as New Orleans without beans and rice, gumbo or po' boys. She lights up the stage with her warm and generous smile, capturing the essence of New Orleans soul and R&B as she second lines, waving a towel or cloth over her head. When Hurricane Katrina hit, rumours quickly spread that Irma had been killed, but Irma was safe in Texas, having just performed in Austin. Her house and club, however, fared much worse; the club was destroyed, and Irma lost all her possessions.

Irma's club, the Lion's Den, was a small and intimate affair in one of the more unsavory neighbourhoods, downtown on Gravier. It would only open when Irma was in town, so Jazz Fest was a sure bet to catch her—because Irma is always at home (not touring) during Jazz Fest. And the Lion's Den was as close to 'at home' as a music club anywhere could offer.

There was nothing more quintessentially New Orleans than a night at the Lion's Den with Irma Thomas. The evening would start with a drink at the bar followed by a buffet-style red beans and rice, home cooked by Irma herself. Irma is a gracious host, disciplined bandleader and memorable singer. She would perform in a very small room for no more than about 40 or 50 people, backed by some of New Orleans' finest musicians, most of whom have stuck with her for the long haul. The Lion's Den, however, must be consigned to fond memories of 'before the storm'; there are no plans to rebuild or replace it.

In 2007, the New Orleans Jazz and Heritage Festival featured Irma Thomas in a tribute to the life and work of the legendary gospel singer, Mahalia Jackson. This was an inspired piece of programming. At the time, I wrote: "Irma Thomas is respectful and restrained ... Dressed in white, this diva of New Orleans rhythm and blues pays homage to the role of the church as central to all African-American music traditions."

Irma is no former church singer plying her church-trained vocals in contemporary blues, soul or jazz. Irma is a regular churchgoer and choir member, and in 2003 she released a gospel album, *Walk around Heaven: New Orleans Gospel Soul*.

The photographs of Irma that work best for me describe either the passion and commitment or the joy and warmth of her secular soul performances. She has built a dedicated and loyal following all over the world, but it continues to be a mystery why greater success and recognition has eluded this very fine artist.

Left top:
Irma Thomas,
New Orleans Jazz and Heritage Festival, 2005

Left Bottom:
Irma Thomas,
New Orleans Jazz and Heritage Festival, 2014

Right:
Irma Thomas, night concert series,
New Orleans Jazz and Heritage Festival, 1994

IRVIN MAYFIELD

Born 23 December, 1977

Irvin Mayfield is a highly respected young New Orleans trumpet player and band leader with the right image, chops and musical intelligence to single him out as the logical successor to Wynton Marsalis as the international ambassador for New Orleans jazz. This status was confirmed in 2003 when he was appointed Cultural Ambassador of the City of New Orleans and State of Louisiana, and he has subsequently continued to carve out a significant niche as a composer, band leader, artistic director and venue promoter.

In 2002, heavily influenced by the role of Wynton Marsalis in New York, he founded the Institute of Jazz Culture at Dillard University and the New Orleans Jazz Orchestra. In 2008 he was appointed Artistic Director of Jazz for the Minnesota Orchestra. He is also the co-founder, with Bill Summers (master percussionist of Headhunters fame), of the award-winning Latin jazz group Los Hombres Calientes. Mayfield is not only jazz-cool, he is also Latin-hip. This is a young man who looks good, sounds great and crosses styles and genres with comfort and élan.

On 19 September 2005, the *New York Times* reviewed the 'Higher Ground' benefit Wynton Marsalis organised for Hurricane Katrina relief in New York with the following observation:

> The concert's most touching moment was a performance by the New Orleans trumpeter Irvin Mayfield. His father, he said, is still among the missing. He played 'Just a Closer Walk with Thee', the hymn that becomes both dirge and celebration at New Orleans funerals. From a hushed, sustained, almost tearful beginning, it turned more assertive and ornate, with growls and extended slides, determined to rise above sorrow.

Mayfield's father's death was subsequently confirmed and the Episcopal Dean of the Christ Church Cathedral in New Orleans commissioned 'All The Saints', an ode to the city which was one of the first major cultural performances in New Orleans after Katrina. Other notable compositions include 'Half Past Autumn Suite', a tribute to American artist Gordon Parks commissioned by the New Orleans Museum of Art, and 'Strange Fruit', documenting the tragic lives of an interracial couple in the 1920s, commissioned by Dillard University.

Mayfield is the whole package. Schooled in the traditions of jazz by Ellis Marsalis, the patriarch of the Marsalis family, Mayfield has the serious talent and commitment of a jazz evangelist. He also swings with the sensitivities of Latin dance and is blessed with stylish good looks—a kind of Creole James Dean.

In a promotional video for the Irvin Mayfield Jazz Playhouse—the second venue in town to carry his name as the draw card—Irvin makes the perfect pitch: "Jazz is in the heart—no, the soul—of those who embrace it. And this city has been seduced by it... Jazz is the art form that speaks directly to the angels." The words Irvin and Mayfield are likely to be synonymous with the words New and Orleans for many years to come.

POSTSCRIPT, MAY 2015

Mayfield's reputation has been called into question by allegations that $863,000 of funds from the New Orleans Public Library Foundation have been transferred to Mayfield's New Orleans Jazz Orchestra (NOJO). Mayfield is a board member of both organisations and is paid a salary by NOJO. NOJO and its Board of Directors have responded by expressing their disappointment in misperceptions and announcing to "aggressively move forward" to "return the dollars from the library foundation and immediately refocus on our mission to put jazz musicians to work, celebrate our culture, and travel the world promoting New Orleans and performing jazz music."

Irvin Mayfield,
New Orleans Jazz and
Heritage Festival, 2003

Left: Irvin Mayfield (and son),
New Orleans Jazz and Heritage Festival, 2005

Irvin Mayfield,
New Orleans Jazz and
Heritage Festival, 2009

Nicholas Payton, New Orleans Jazz and Heritage Festival, 2010

NICHOLAS PAYTON
Born 26 September, 1973

Back in 1994, at the tender age of 21, Nicholas Payton was put in the extraordinary position of being identified by the octogenarian trumpeter, Doc Cheatham, as the reincarnation of the legendary King Oliver. This was a young man who already had the pedigree to become one of the next great trumpeters from the home of some of the most important trumpet players in jazz history. The son of the highly respected New Orleans bass player Walter Payton, Nicholas played in the Tuxedo Brass Band at the age of ten and toured throughout the USA and Europe at twelve.

It has been intriguing to watch Nicholas grow up amid such high expectations. He is without any shadow of a doubt a very fine musician with an exceptional tone and feel. You could always sense the reverence for the history of the music he holds in his trumpet. And as he ages, he radiates on stage a sense of maturity, poise, presence and status.

Significant collaborations include Ray Charles, Daniel Lanois, Dr. John, Roy Haynes, Joe Henderson, Clark Terry, Allen Toussaint, Chucho Valdes, Dr. Michael White and Nancy Wilson. His 1997 recording with Doc Cheatham

won them a Grammy award for best jazz instrumental solo. In 2011, he wrote an extraordinary piece that pronounced jazz dead. Rejecting the jazz label as a moribund marketing device, he had this to say of his earlier collaboration:

> Some may say that I'm no longer the same dude who recorded the album with Doc Cheatham.
>
> Correct: I'm not the same dude I was 14 years ago.
>
> Isn't that the point?
>
> Our whole purpose on this planet is to evolve.
>
> The Golden Age of Jazz is gone.

One of my favorite comments in this deliberately provocative piece is his reflection on silence, which I also write about in reference to Miles Davis. Payton says of Miles: "Miles Davis personified cool and he hated jazz". Payton says of silence:

> Silence is music, too.
>
> ...
>
> It's where you choose to put silence that makes sound music.
>
> Sound and silence equals music.
>
> Sometimes when I'm soloing, I don't play shit.
>
> I just move blocks of silence around.
>
> The notes are an afterthought.
>
> Silence is what makes music sexy.
>
> Silence is cool.

Subsequent writing under the moniker 'Nicholas Payton aka The Saviour of Archaic Pop', he adopts equally provocative and confronting views, particularly on race relations. This, for example, from December 2014, on the latest release by D'Angelo: "I can't get with Black people who play Rock. Rock is the White appropriation of the Blues. The Blues didn't need another name. There is no need to mimic the voice of the oppressor back to him."

When I think about Nicholas, I remember a simple onstage gesture he made as a young man back in 1994. It has stuck in my mind ever since. Unfortunately, I wasn't ready to take the photograph—I think I may have been changing a roll of film—and I haven't seen him repeat the gesture since. Somehow, however, this simple but moving tribute summed up everything that could be said about this young man. He laid the trumpet across the flat of both palms, and held the instrument out in front of him, almost as if he was making an offering to, or acknowledging, a higher power. Or perhaps he knew then what he would later write in 2011:

> I am a part of a lineage.
> I am a part of a blood line.
>
> My ancestors didn't play Jazz, they played Traditional, Modern and Avant-garde New Orleans Music.
>
> I don't play Jazz.
>
> I don't let others define who I am.
>
> I am a Postmodern New Orleans musician.

Nicholas Payton,
New Orleans Jazz and Heritage Festival, 2008

Snooks Eaglin, New Orleans Jazz and Heritage Festival, 2007

Snooks Eaglin, New Orleans Jazz and Heritage Festival, 2004

SNOOKS EAGLIN
21 January, 1936/37 – 18 February, 2009

Snooks was such a familiar and reassuring figure on the New Orleans music scene that his passing in February 2009 came as a real shock. His irrepressible energy made it seem as if he was immortal, although the truth of it was that he had been diagnosed with prostate cancer in 2008.

His guitar style was unique. He confounded musicians, critics and fans throughout his career. He didn't pick or strum; his fingers flailed at the strings, the top joints seeming to bend back at unnatural angles. At the same time, his thumb would pick out the bass lines. Snooks, it seemed, could play lead, bass, and rhythm at the same time.

He earned the nickname 'the human jukebox' from his extraordinarily wide repertoire of material, said to be in the order of 2,500 songs. He was comfortable in a range of styles including blues, rock, jazz, country and Latin and had a legendary ability to pick up on a song and play it perfectly on first hearing.

Over the years he recorded with many of the major artists in New Orleans—'Sugar Boy' Crawford, Allen Toussaint, James Booker, Ellis Marsalis, Professor Longhair, Henry Butler and Earl King to name a few—cementing his place as one of the pivotal musicians from the era spanning the second half of the last century.

Born Fird Eaglin, Jr., he lost his sight at the age of 19 months following an operation on a brain tumour, but this did not slow him down. In OffBeat Magazine's 2009 obituary, Snooks is quoted on the origin of his name: "There was a radio program with a character named Baby Snooks. Baby Snooks was always getting into trouble. They started calling me Snooks, because I was always getting into something." He certainly didn't look anything like his 73 years of age, and he was always "getting into something" at his Jazz Festival and Rock 'n' Bowl gigs. You could never be sure just where the concert might be going as Snooks would reach back into his vast repertoire to respond to requests from his devoted fans or follow a momentary whim.

The Mid City Lanes Rock 'n' Bowl was a unique New Orleans venue in a dilapidated hall that housed a bowling lane and concert venue upstairs, and for a few years prior to Katrina, a second concert hall downstairs. No visit to New Orleans was complete without a blues or zydeco night at the Rock 'n' Bowl, and no better night could be had than a Snooks Eaglin concert.

The Rock 'n' Bowl moved to a new purpose-built venue in April 2009, shortly after Eaglin's death. The two events are unrelated but it is notable that none of the old guard of New Orleans blues men—Snooks Eaglin, Johnny Adams and Earl King—lived to perform in the new venue. It may have improved its facilities, but possibly at the cost of its soul.

Trombone Shorty, New Orleans Jazz and Heritage Festival, 2011

TROY 'TROMBONE SHORTY' ANDREWS
Born 2 January, 1986

Trombone Shorty was always going to be a major figure in the trombone and trumpet history of New Orleans. Hailing from Treme, the hotbed of brass band culture in the city, he is the younger brother of James Andrews, the 'Satchmo of the Ghetto'. Photographs of Trombone Shorty as a young boy with an unwieldy instrument were no cute affectation; he was a bandleader at the age of six and has been a key figure in the development of New Orleans brass music for at least a decade.

His current incarnation is a brass funk hip-hop outfit drawing on his background as a graduate of the prestigious New Orleans Center for the Creative Arts. 'Orleans Avenue' is a dynamic live performance outfit that dub their music 'SupaFunkRock', and have built a reputation for high-energy concerts that few other artists could keep up with. Their increasing acceptance into the mainstream is built on their dynamic performances and high-profile collaborations with artists such as Lenny Kravitz, U2, Diana Krall, Norah Jones and Juvenile.

Trombone Shorty has this uncanny mix of ability and charisma that means he always adds something to any gig he works—and work he does. On any night he is likely to be sitting in or guesting on what seems like just about every gig in town.

It may seem odd that my preferred photograph of Trombone Shorty does not feature a trombone. He is, however, an extraordinarily talented multi-instrumentalist and in later years the trumpet has become his preferred instrument, although he still regularly plays the trombone in a variety of settings.

The afternoon at Jazz Fest back in 2005 (about four months prior to Katrina) when he picked up two horns and kept a packed jazz tent captivated not only produced a memorable image, it marked the coming of age of this young performer as a musical leader of maturity and substance in his own right. Since then, and in part due to the confidence he developed while touring with Lenny Kravitz in that same year, Trombone Shorty has become the leading light of the new generation of New Orleans musicians.

The future of New Orleans music depends on family dynasties and heartland neighbourhoods building new traditions on the old. Trombone Shorty is the face and sound of that future.

Trombone Shorty,
New Orleans Jazz and
Heritage Festival, 2015

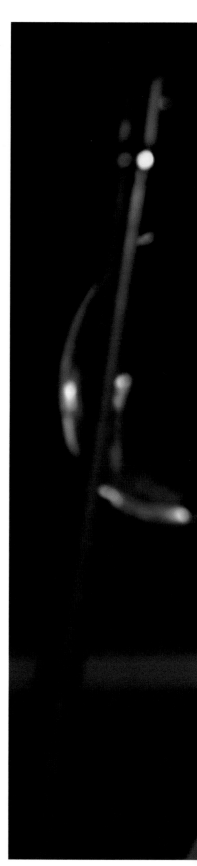

Trombone Shorty,
New Orleans Jazz and
Heritage Festival, 2004

WYNTON MARSALIS
Born 18 October, 1961

Wynton Marsalis, widely recognized as the international face of contemporary modern jazz, is arguably the most influential jazz musician of his generation. He is an advocate, an educator, and a very, very fine trumpet player.

Through his current roles in New York as Artistic Director at the Jazz at Lincoln Center and Music Director of the Jazz at Lincoln Center Orchestra he has, almost single-handedly, carried the torch for the recognition of jazz music as a major American art form. He has however, been criticized over the years as self-serving, conservative and unadventurous; replicating the masters and standards without moving the music forward.

I have always thought the criticisms unjustified—and the basis for this view begins with the exceptional tone of Marsalis' trumpet. It is as clear and pure as any living trumpeter I have heard, and because of this clarity of tone it is, to my ear, inherently evocative. It also lends itself to the time-honored tradition of respectfully reworking jazz standards as an integral part of the evolution of jazz music. You could choose to interpret such a pure and deferential trumpet sound as derivative and uninteresting. Or you could enjoy it for what it is, and hear it as the starting point for an exploration of the full range of human emotions and experience.

In most English-speaking countries outside the USA, the kind of criticisms levelled at Marsalis would be considered classic examples of the 'tall poppy syndrome', because the criticisms are aimed at cutting a prominent personality down to size, bringing him back to everyone else's level. The problem with the tall poppy syndrome, to misquote a literary reference, is that some poppies really are taller than others.

I have been fortunate to see Wynton Marsalis perform and speak on numerous occasions. I have never found him constrained by tradition. He has always been informative, engaging and entertaining. He is passionately committed to the unfinished struggle for the recognition of jazz as one of the most important new art forms of the twentieth century, and he carries this cultural crusade with an appropriate mix of humility and pride.

Marsalis understands that standards, classics and traditions, in any genre or art form, do not stand still; they move and evolve over time, responding to, and influencing, the context within which this evolution takes place. Deference and humility in acknowledging those traditions is not stifling or anti-creative. Handled sensitively and respectfully, reaching back to the past to provide nuances and emphases for the future can be hugely satisfying and rewarding, and, in the right hands, exciting and scintillating.

Marsalis also understands that different traditions and histories can interact in new and exciting ways. On the opening day of the 2009 New Orleans Jazz and Heritage Festival, on what is known as the Congo stage, traditionally reserved for soul, reggae, African and hip-hop acts, Wynton Marsalis and the Jazz at Lincoln Center Orchestra teamed up with Yacub Addy's Ghanaian music troupe, Odadaa!, to perform 'Congo Square', a two-hour composition by Marsalis and Addy commissioned in the aftermath of Hurricane Katrina. It was first performed in Congo Square in New Orleans on 23 April 2006. The complex layers of meaning associated with this collaboration of an African traditionalist and an African-American upholder of tradition, and the choice of Congo Square—the birthplace of the unique cultural and musical contributions of New Orleans—for both the composition's title and the location for its premiere in 2006, are somehow all captured within the opening notes played by the trumpet of Marsalis.

I was not there to hear this call of the trumpet in 2006, but I did hear it in 2009. Marsalis' opening solo must surely dispel all doubts and reservations about his playing. If anything could destroy the myth that Marsalis lacks emotion and depth, surely it was this: a plaintive and moving clarion call capturing loss and sorrow, hope and despair, renewal and rebirth, the past and the future. This was as soulful and moving as anything I have ever heard, full of pain and anguish, but with a muted hope matched by the bowler-hat-shaped mute Marsalis uses to stretch and expand the notes.

Wynton Marsalis, New Orleans Jazz and Heritage Festival, 2009

Wynton and Ellis Marsalis, New Orleans Jazz and Heritage Festival,1996

Wynton Marsalis, New Orleans Jazz and Heritage Festival, circa 1995

Wynton Marsalis, New Orleans Jazz and Heritage Festival, circa 1995

I do not think I was alone that afternoon in shedding a tear for the suffering and loss of Marsalis' home city, a city that so many visitors from all corners of the globe have come to know and love; a city that has woven its fabric, its rhythm and its culture into every aspect of popular Western culture—even if most people who subscribe to its influences are unaware of the origins back in Congo Square.

This extraordinary Marsalis/Addy collaboration is nothing less than a conscious step towards redefining the place of jazz in American and world music. By his own account, Marsalis has been undertaking a search for what he calls the real American rhythm. He believes that the back-beat of rock 'n' roll—a New Orleans innovation—has placed too many restrictions on American music. It has locked the music of the United States in a perpetual cycle suited to dance, but unsuited to the more sophisticated storytelling that goes with African rhythms.

Marsalis and Addy's epic two-hour journey signposted a new relationship between the musical cultures of two intrinsically interlinked continents, through the marriage of the studied technique of a jazz orchestra and the rolling poly-rhythms of African storytellers. At the conclusion of the performance, the orchestra marches offstage with the African musicians. As the musicians leave the stage, the fading sound of drums and horns, no longer amplified, trails away into a series of unanswered questions.

I for one am convinced that so long as Wynton Marsalis continues to ask the questions, the jazz tradition is in safe hands. The worry for me will be when Marsalis (or others) either no longer ask the questions, or become convinced that they already know the answers.

Yacub Addy,
New Orleans Jazz and
Heritage Festival, 2009

Wynton Marsalis with
Yacub Addy's Odadaa!,
New Orleans Jazz and
Heritage Festival, 2009

Herb Hardesty and Dr. John, WWOZ Piano Night, New Orleans, 2003

Charmaine Neville, New Orleans Jazz and Heritage Festival, 1996

Deacon John,
New Orleans Jazz and
Heritage Festival, 2011

Anders Osborne,
New Orleans Jazz and
Heritage Festival, 2011

Chris Owens (on right), New Orleans Jazz and Heritage Festival, 2009

Washboard Chaz at Chaz Fest, New Orleans, 2011

Big Chief Monk Boudreaux and Irvin Mayfield, New Orleans Jazz and Heritage Festival, 2012

Big Sam entertaining extras at the filming of the TV program, Treme, during New Orleans Jazz and Heritage Festival, 2011

Christian Scott, New Orleans Jazz and Heritage Festival, 2011

Davell Crawford, New Orleans Jazz and Heritage Festival, 2014

Ellis Marsalis,
New Orleans Jazz and
Heritage Festival, 2011

Delfeayo Marsalis,
New Orleans Jazz and
Heritage Festival, 2011

Gregg Stafford leads the Young Tuxedo Brass Band, New Orleans Jazz and Heritage Festival, 2011

Earl Palmer
performing at the first
Ponderosa Stomp,
New Orleans, 2002

Johnny Vidacovich,
New Orleans Jazz and
Heritage Festival, 2011

John Boutte,
New Orleans Jazz and
Heritage Festival, 2011

Jon Cleary,
New Orleans Jazz and
Heritage Festival, 2014

Marva Wright,
New Orleans Jazz and
Heritage Festival, 1996

Rebirth Brass Band,
Tipitina's New Orleans, 2004

Kermit Ruffins,
New Orleans Jazz and
Heritage Festival, 2012

Top Left to Right: Ellis Marsalis WWOZ Piano Night, New Orleans, 2014; Pete Fountain, New Orleans Jazz and Heritage Festival, 1994; Walter "Wolfman" Washington, New Orleans Jazz and Heritage Festival, 2007; Terence Blanchard, New Orleans Jazz and Heritage Festival, 2000

Bottom Left to Right: Helen Gillet and the Other Instruments at Chaz Fest, New Orleans, 2015; The Tin Men at dba club, Frenchmen Street, New Orleans, 2014; Lloyd Washington at Anita's Diner, New Orleans, 1994; Theresa Andersson, New Orleans Jazz and Heritage Festival, 2010; Coco Robicheaux, New Orleans Jazz and Heritage Festival, 2001; Ernie K Doe, New Orleans Jazz and Heritage Festival, 2000

SOUL
ARTISTS

Ray Charles, Blackpool, 1992

AL GREEN
Born 13 April, 1946

Live on stage, Al Green has no peer. He is far and away the most exciting live performer I have ever seen. This is not a singular view—several of my colleagues with a collective exposure to thousands of live concerts and artists all agree: nothing beats the Reverend Al Green on form. Even a bad Al Green gig (although I'm not sure there is such a thing) is better than most other live performers will ever achieve in a lifetime.

There is electricity and dynamism to Al Green that is joyously uplifting, exciting and thrilling, emotional and moving, all at the same time. You just don't know what he is going to do next, or where he is going to take you, but you sure want to go along for the ride! He can be in glorious full flow, deep into one of his soulful masterpieces—perhaps 'Take Me to the River', or 'I'm Still in Love with You'—and then he will shift gear, mid-chorus, and take the music on some extravagant tangent, or segue to another of his hits, perhaps 'I Can't Get Next to You', 'Let's Stay Together' or 'Tired of Being Alone'. The element that holds this together is his nervous energy and excitement, and, of course, that voice—the deepest soul and the purest gospel, soaring and flying, whispering and crooning. He always has great musicians—they have to be—because they have to keep up with him. They have to be able to change gear and rhythm mid-song, and stay close to the man as he takes the audience on whatever flight of fancy takes him.

Justin Timberlake wrote a piece in *Rolling Stone* (April 15, 2004) after Al Green was voted number 65 in their list of 100 all-time greatest artists. Timberlake, no slouch in the performance stakes, acknowledged that "These days, everything is about the show. But Al Green is the show, and when you watch him perform, you get to see something honest and soulful and amazing." He also says that "Al Green has helped overpopulate the world. He's got some serious babymaking music. But what makes him such an inspiration is the raw passion, the sincerity and the joy he brings to his music."

Green's career has followed turbulent paths, mirroring his larger than life personality, and not unlike the roller-coaster ride of an Al Green concert. He was one of the most important and popular soul singers of the early '70s, but his R&B career slipped when he became ordained as pastor of the Full Gospel Tabernacle in Memphis in 1976. He went on to concentrate on gospel for the better part of the 1980s, winning no less than eight Grammys in that period.

He returned to R&B in 1998 with a duet with Annie Lennox for the 1998 Bill Murray film Scrooged, and has continued to release soul records since that time, regularly appearing on the international festival and concert circuit, including Jazz Fest. He was inducted into the Rock and Roll Hall of Fame in 1995 and the Gospel Music Hall of Fame in 2004. He received a Grammy Lifetime Achievement Award in 2002, and a BET (Black Entertainment Television) Lifetime Achievement Award in 2008.

From my perspective, as a photographer and unreconstructed Al Green fan, I always found it difficult to get a definitive live picture of the man. It wasn't hard to get a strong image—such was the strength and vitality of his show—but I always wanted to get an image which would somehow define him. In 2004, the opportunity arose at the Saenger Theatre in New Orleans. Green was on fire, he was bursting out of his skin, jumping around on stage like a newborn kangaroo on speed. I made my way to front of stage right and Green, as is his want at every live gig, was showering the crowd with sprays of single red roses. He moved to the front of stage left, and I pressed the shutter. To the best of my ability, I had finally come as close as I could to capturing what it was like to be there, luxuriating in the sheer joy and pleasure of Al Green, live on stage.

Al Green, Saenger Theatre, New Orleans, 2004

Al Green,
Royal Festival Hall,
London, circa 1992

Al Green,
New Orleans Jazz and
Heritage Festival, 1995

ARETHA FRANKLIN
Born 25 March, 1942

Aretha Franklin, the "Queen of Soul", is deservedly one of the most acclaimed singers alive today. Ranked first on the *Rolling Stone* list of greatest singers of all time and ninth on their list of all-time great artists, she has topped the Billboard R&B charts on 20 occasions, won 18 Grammy Awards and in 1987, became the first woman to be inducted into the Rock and Roll Hall of Fame. She was awarded the National Medal of Arts by President Clinton in 1999, the Presidential Medal of Freedom by President Bush in 2005 and was the featured vocalist at the inauguration of President Obama on 20 January 2009. This last honor was widely regarded, by Franklin's virtually peerless standards, as a lacklustre performance, and might be read as symbolic of her career which has fluctuated over the years in terms of both popular success and critical acclaim.

It was her string of hits in the '60s and '70s for Atlantic Records, 'Respect', 'I Never Loved a Man', 'Chain of Fools', 'Baby I Love You', 'I Say a Little Prayer', 'Think', and 'The House That Jack Built', that indelibly stamped Aretha Franklin as one of the most influential voices in the history of popular music. I was privileged to see Aretha Franklin perform twice, once in the day and once at night, at the New Orleans Jazz and Heritage Festival in 1994. In a review of the festival published in Australia's *Good Weekend* magazine in 1994, I wrote that "B.B. King sets up an ecstatic crowd for a rare Aretha Franklin outing: the Queen of Soul is the highlight of the festival, with power and stature that set her apart as a vocalist of rare talent."

The night performance was considerably more memorable than the day performance, which was somehow more homey and casual by comparison. Perhaps it was the resplendent red evening gown, or the sense of occasion of going out for an Aretha Franklin concert, but whatever it was, Aretha was transcendent. In person, and on song, her vocal is rich and warm, smooth and sweet, soulful and spiritual, all at the same time. You can hear and feel the gospel roots that have given birth to so many great soul singers, including of course, the Queen herself.

Aretha Franklin has been billed to perform at Jazz Fest on two subsequent occasions, each time pulling out at the last minute. One of those times was in 2009, when the story circulating around town was that she did not want to risk her health or her voice as news of the BP oil spill in the Gulf of Mexico began to grab the attention of national and international media.

It is a measure of the woman that she need only be called by her first name for people to immediately know to whom you are referring. No one else has so comprehensively and effectively managed to combine gospel, soul, blues and jazz into such mass popularity. Her biggest hit, the 1967 reworking of an Otis Redding song, stands out as the high water mark of her career and remains her personal anthem: 'Respect'.

Left and Right:
Aretha Franklin,
New Orleans Jazz and
Heritage Festival, 1994

EARTH WIND AND FIRE

My estimation of Barack Obama, already high due to his visionary presidential campaign and his credentials as a writer of considerable quality, rose again when I learned that he chose Earth, Wind & Fire to perform at the first formal White House dinner hosted by the new president and the first lady in February 2009. This was not the first time Earth Wind and Fire had wowed the White House; they performed at a Bill Clinton dinner for the King of Morocco in June 2000, and on the back of that performance, King Mohammed VI invited them to perform at his birthday celebration in Morocco later that same year.

The awards and accolades for Earth Wind and Fire include induction into the Rock and Roll Hall of Fame (2000) and Vocal Group Hall of Fame (2003), and a star on the Hollywood Walk of Fame in 1995. They have won ten Grammy Awards and four American Music Awards and are the seventh biggest-selling American band of all time.

The *Rolling Stone Encyclopaedia of Rock & Roll* (Simon & Schuster, 2001) describes them as "Innovative yet popular, precise yet sensual, calculated yet galvanizing, Earth, Wind & Fire changed the sound of black pop in the '70s." What has always stood out for me is the larger than life sound, the grand and lustrous harmonies and vocal interplay, the quality of the production, and, above all, the horn arrangements. Along with James Brown's horn sections, the Phoenix Horns has set the standards by which all other R&B, groove or dance-oriented horn sections must subsequently be measured.

I wasn't around to witness the big stadium performances of the 1970s, with pyrotechnics and vanishing pyramids, but I was fortunate enough to be the lone photographer (or perhaps one of only two, I can't quite remember) in the photo-pit of a night concert at the New Orleans Jazz and Heritage Festival in 1997. And I had wisely brought with me a fast wide-angle lens (from memory I think either a 17 or 19mm). The band's performance was as golden as the resulting photographs. I couldn't have stage managed a better performance for a wide-angle lens at the center and front of stage.

When I next saw Earth Wind and Fire, it was in 2009, at a daytime concert in the 2009 Jazz and Heritage Festival. The pictures just didn't seem to be working—maybe it was because the band wasn't as tight or lively as twelve years before, or maybe it was because they were wearing white (the most difficult color for photographing black artists), or maybe it was because the light was all over the place as the sun moved in and out of cloud cover. Sometimes, however, you know it just really doesn't matter, because you know you will never get better pictures of the artist than those you have shot before, and for Earth Wind and Fire, for me, there will never be another concert like 1997 at the UNO Lakefront Arena.

Left and Right: Earth Wind and Fire, New Orleans Jazz and Heritage Festival, 1997

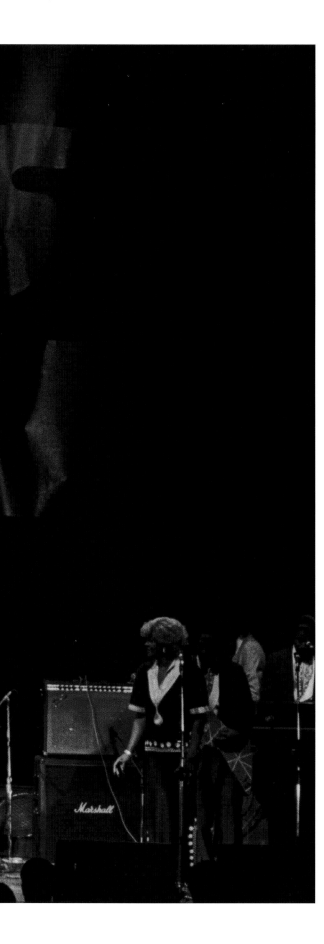

JAMES BROWN
3 May, 1933 – 25 December, 2006

There was only ever one 'Godfather of Soul', but you can also take your pick from a range of more or less accurate epithets including 'King of Soul', 'Soul Brother Number One', 'Mr. Dynamite', 'The Hardest-Working Man in Show Business', 'The King of Funk' and 'Minister of the New Super Heavy Funk'. I saw James Brown perform on many occasions, but none more important (photographically at least) than the Hammersmith Odeon in London on 23 May 1985. This was a memorable concert with a stage set-up that included a series of full-size backdrops—including JAMES BROWN in huge letters and a stylized New York night skyline. James was on fire—one of the most electric and athletic performances I ever saw. Although I had seen him perform a few years earlier at a San Francisco nightclub, this was the first concert of his that I photographed, and he was naturally in better condition than at later gigs when age began to slow him down (but only just!)

At this London concert, he pulled out every trick in the book—his trademark moves, turns, walks and leaps, and his mesmerizing microphone work. Nobody could animate a microphone stand quite like James Brown—in his hands it became an object of devotion, a ballroom dancing partner—the straight fall guy (or gal) to Brown's extravagant showmanship. I can't remember who I was working for at the time, but I do recall I was only permitted front-of-stage access for a couple of numbers; at that point, Brown was barely warming up. I took a seat at the rear of the hall, joining my then partner. We watched the rest of the gig with my six-month-old son fast asleep on our laps. Yes, he has the rare privilege of being able to say that he slept through a James Brown concert in 1985!

As the concert unfolded and the backdrops changed, I took photographs from behind the sound desk, alternating between camera bodies with black and white and color film. The 1/125th of a second (the shutter speed I would have been using at the time) that would capture the shot of the night—James Brown spread-eagled in mid-air—coincided with the black and white body. I've always been surprised why this picture hasn't been published more often (maybe it would have had more currency in color) but of all the pictures I have taken, this is probably the one that most people would like to own.

At subsequent James Brown concerts, for example at an outdoor concert in south London in 1994, James could still thrill with a great show. He could still do all his great numbers—'Papa's Got a Brand New Bag', 'Got You (I Feel Good)', 'Funky Drummer', 'It's a Man's World', 'Please, Please, Please', 'Say It Loud – I'm Black and I'm Proud', 'Get Up (I Feel Like Being a) Sex Machine'—and he could still make all the right moves (or more than enough to indicate what they might have once been); but he had lost the athleticism, joy and spontaneity from ten years earlier.

There is a sure sign that an elder statesman of the American music industry has settled for the formulaic performance of the comfortable and lucrative touring circuit that originates in the casinos of Las Vegas. When the headline artist doesn't come on stage until 30 to 60 minutes into the show, what you will be getting is a pre-packaged formula that ticks all the boxes, without ever scaling the heights that the artist might have originally become known for. It is not a sell-out and it is not a rip-off, it is just not what it could be; but for most artists at this stage of their careers, just the thrill of seeing them live is enough for most fans.

One of the downsides of being a music photographer is that you are often so intently focused on getting the picture that you miss the music. I try to make a point of enjoying the music, and I am regularly the lone photographer in the pit moving to the music or applauding a solo, but sometimes you know that you are recording history and the object of the evening becomes a quest for the definitive image. I remember a friend of mine asking what I thought of James Brown's bass player while we were making our way home from the 1994 gig. The truth of it was that he may as well not have had one—I could have described every nuance of Brown's face, or every flick of his overly manicured hair. I could just about have named every sequin on his red waistcoat, but his band: not a chance. One of the ironies of this is that it took a revival of interest in soul and groove dance music in the late 1980s to remind me just how great James Brown's musicians were. In particular, the JB Horns, Brown's phenomenal horn section from the backing band of the '60s and '70s, headlined their own sell-out gigs in London in the late 1980s and early 1990s. With Maceo Parker and Pee Wee Ellis on saxophone, and Fred Wesley on trombone, the JB Horns redefined the standards for horn sections working in the dance cross-over genres of jazz, soul and funk.

James Brown's career has been acknowledged by a string of honors including a lifetime achievement award at the 34th Grammy Awards, induction into the Rock and Roll Hall of Fame, the New York Songwriters Hall of Fame and the UK Music Hall of Fame, and a star on

James Brown, Hammersmith Odeon, London 1985

the Hollywood Walk of Fame. His home town of Augusta, Georgia has honored him with a statue and a civic arena carrying his name. In Colorado, local residents voted to name a bridge over the Yampa River the 'James Brown Soul Center of the Universe Bridge'. I suspect however, that the most accurate measure of his legacy to contemporary music and culture is the river of sweat from late-night clubbers all over the world as they "get on down" while James Brown "gets on up"; surely there is no other artist on this planet more guaranteed to get a dance floor jumping than James Brown.

Left and Below: James Brown, Hammersmith Odeon, London, 1985

James Brown, Crystal Palace, London, 1994

RAY CHARLES
23 September, 1930 – 10 June, 2004

There was only ever one 'Brother Ray' and I was fortunate enough to see him perform on three separate occasions: once in Blackpool and twice in New Orleans. He was a consummate professional with the highest of expectations for his immaculately drilled big bands.

I remember at Blackpool, in the English summer of 1992, that his drummer turned up late for the gig. The band somehow winged it through the first number while the English drummer in Ronnie Scott's support band—Martin Drew— held out for an outrageously high fee to sit in and save the gig. Ray's drummer finally turned up as the second number began—he had slept late in his hotel room—and slipped into the chair, I suspect unnoticed by the audience. As the drummer (whose name escapes me) told me the following day, Ray was furious, telling him in no uncertain terms: "I'm blind and I could make the gig on time!"

Ray's sound was always lush and full—his vocals could easily handle everything from the deepest soul and the most spiritual gospel to schmaltzy pop ballads. His stage persona was electric in its intensity—he always looked great and put on a great show. His signature move—hard to capture in photographs (because it is hard to hold focus)—was to throw this head back in abandon as his right hand pounded the keyboard. He also had this way of standing at the keyboard and bending forward, almost as if he was physically transported into the joyous moment of musical creation.

Much more has been said, and can be said, about his influence and musical genius, and his ability to reinvent musical genres, take them to new audiences and make them his own. I will always cherish the memory of his live energy, and it was both humbling and gratifying when *The Economist* magazine chose one of my images to illustrate their obituary of June 19, 2004. The line I like best from that particular obituary is "Mr. Charles did not invent 'soul', as he came to call it. But he put his stamp on it so thoroughly ... that he may as well have done."

Ray Charles,
New Orleans Jazz and
Heritage Festival, 1995

ROY AYERS
Born 10 September, 1940

Roy Ayers is a very fine jazz musician who played with Herbie Mann in the 60s, Fela Kuti in the 70s, and then helped define jazz funk, acid jazz and jazz hip hop club dance music into the 80s and 90s. In person, Roy Ayers is a remarkably warm and generous person—he lives up to the expectations created by his music. He makes you comfortable and welcome in his presence, and maintains a laudable mix of professionalism and selflessness in his approach to concerts, media and fans. He is also one of those musicians who tends to slip under the mainstream radar, but gets rediscovered with every new genre or movement that looks back to the rich history of jazz, soul and R&B.

I first came across Roy Ayers in the late 1980s and early 1990s when groove dance music was building in popularity in the United Kingdom. Ayers had already been picked up by the northern soul clubs in regional England, but he was rapidly becoming a mainstay of London clubs and radio DJs, attracted by his cool, mellow and groove-ful tunes. Some of his recordings became dance classics, including 'Running Away', 'Sweet Tears', 'Can't You See Me' and 'Love Will Bring Us Back Together'. 'Everybody Loves the Sunshine' became the soundtrack to the rare English summer treasure of golden days and evenings; it captured the fleeting pleasure of long summer afternoons and evenings in an otherwise grey and dreary London. "Folks get down in the sunshine ... Everybody loves the sunshine."

I met Roy Ayers in 1992, when he was performing at the Blackpool Jazz Festival. He was the consummate gentleman and the consummate performer. He was hobbling around with the aid of a walking stick, having recently injured his knee. There was, however, nothing that was too much trouble. He was accommodating with studio-lit photographs backstage before the gig, and I recall he was very loving with his wife who accompanied him on tour. The set was memorable—he played with style and verve, performing all his hit songs with incredible energy, which he somehow managed to maintain while remaining seated at his vibraphone for the night. Maybe this made it easier for me to photograph him—he certainly couldn't move around too much!

I don't know too much about the jazz and hip-hop dance movement in the 90s, but I am not surprised that Roy Ayers was at its center, or thereabouts. What Roy Ayers has accomplished is the skill and foresight to bring his jazz sensitivities to the R&B and soul scenes, and, in the process, create some timeless grooves. These have influenced subsequent dance genres and will continue to do so, because the desire to dance is universal across generations.

I last saw Roy Ayers in a small Melbourne (Australia) jazz club in 2015. He was as soulful as he always has been, but perhaps even more funky. There was also a new element of the sage philosopher I hadn't recalled: "Let your mind be free ... I'm just trying to give you music to let you look to the sky."

Left and Below: Roy Ayers, Blackpool, 1992

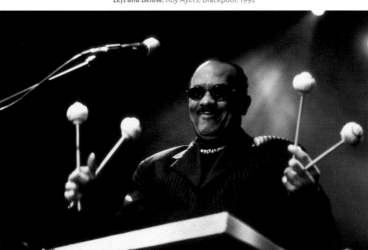

Erykah Badu, New Orleans Jazz and Heritage Festival, 2009

Bobby Womack, New Orleans Jazz and Heritage Festival, 2014

Estelle,
New Orleans Jazz and
Heritage Festival, 2015

Anthony Hamilton
New Orleans Jazz and
Heritage Festival, 2015

Maceo Parker, New Orleans Jazz and Heritage Festival, 2011

Pee Wee Ellis
and Maceo Parker
New Orleans Jazz and
Heritage Festival, 2011

Percy Sledge,
New Orleans Jazz and
Heritage Festival, 2007

Bottom Left to right: Chuck Brown, New Orleans Jazz and Heritage Festival, 2009; Smokey Robinson, New Orleans Jazz and Heritage Festival, 2004; Jimmy Smith, New Orleans, 2004
Teddy Pendergrass, New Orleans Jazz and Heritage Festival, 2002; Isaac Hayes, New Orleans Jazz and Heritage Festival, 2005

JAZZ ARTISTS

Nina Simone, Blackpool, 1992

AHMAD JAMAL
Born 2 July, 1930

Ahmad Jamal is one of the most influential jazz pianists in modern jazz. He plays and composes with a lightness of touch and a sensitivity to time and tone that hallmarks him as one of the all-time great band leader of small ensembles. Jamal prefers the term small ensemble to a trio, because it more accurately represents his orchestral approach and his penchant for adding additional instrumentation to the basic bass, drums and piano unit which has been at the center of the body of work he has produced over 50 years.

Miles Davis was one of many senior jazz figures who credit Jamal as a major influence. Miles was an open admirer of Jamal, but although they lived for a time just a block and a half from each other, they were destined to never play or record together—because, as Jamal has explained, they were band leaders at the same time. Their mutual respect and admiration, however, is clearly apparent in their parallel explorations of time, space and tone.

Jamal is probably best known for his definitive version of the jazz standard, 'Poinciana' which was included on the album *At the Pershing: But Not for Me.* This album, recorded live at the Pershing Hotel in Chicago in 1958, remained in the charts for over two years and is widely regarded as one of the classic jazz records of the twentieth century. Jamal is rightly proud of his contribution to what he describes as the only musical form to have originated in the USA and which is emulated all over the world. He has been honored with the National Endowment of the Arts American Jazz Masters Award and is a Duke Ellington Fellow at Yale University.

In June 2007 he was inducted into the prestigious Order of the Arts and Letters by the French Government, an honor that speaks volumes for the role of the French in supporting American jazz musicians, who have historically gained more respect and recognition in Europe than at home in the USA. It also helps to explain why Jamal has such a close affinity with Paris and does most of his recording in Paris or the south of France.

When I photographed Jamal in the early 1990s it was at a sound check in London's Union Chapel. This was an old church converted to a music venue in north London, and for a year or two, whoever did the bookings made it the hippest venue in town for jazz and world music artists. From my recollection of this period, Ahmad Jamal was the only artist who specifically required there be no concert photography.

I was hanging around at the afternoon sound-check with a couple of other photographers I recognized (but didn't know), not sure whether we would be allowed to take photographs. When the band turned up, it was very clear that they were more than a little suspicious and very wary of the photographers in wait. As a group, photographers can't seem to help themselves from behaving like desperate predators,

Left and Right: Ahmad Jamal, Union Chapel, London, circa 1993

cornering their prey and moving in for the kill. It probably has something to do with us all knowing that there is usually just one fraction of a second that each of us is aspiring to capture, and if we are not alert to the possibilities, we might go home empty-handed.

I recall it went something like this. They asked us who we were and what we were doing. They appeared very reluctant to let us take pictures and unconvinced of the need to pander to London media. I was quietly getting ready to pack up my camera bag and leave when the bass player, a tall and statuesque man, whose name I regret I have mislaid, pointed at my camera. "Is that a Leica?" he asked. "Sure is," I responded, "a Leica M4, a rangefinder—the quietest camera I can find for shooting jazz." "In that case," he replied, this time with a broad smile and an expansive wave, "shoot away."

The band got on with their sound check, and I got on with my photographs. I think the other two photographers rode on my coat-tails and got their shots also. In retrospect, I think the musicians might have been jiving all along, and may always have intended to let us take photographs after first giving us a hard time. It might have been a bit of a game with them while on tour. I guess I will never know.

Either way, the pictures I took that day were memorable for the quality of light and the framing, made easier because getting the right angles did not mean upsetting any paying audience members. I like to think these images capture a certain quality of light, space and form that mirrors Jamal's playing. Certainly they were taken with reverence and respect, and I hope this shows.

Years later, in 2011, Jamal performed at Jazz Fest. I had a copy with me of a sample design of this book. I asked the stage manager to take Jamal a copy of the book and to ask if he could tell me the name of the bass player behind him at the London gig. Just prior to Jamal coming on stage, the stage manager returned with the book and told me Jamal had enjoyed the pictures. He told me the name of the bass player, but I guess I am destined to be chasing his name for evermore, as I somehow managed to lose the notebook in which I had written it down. The stage manager also told me Jamal had invited me backstage after the gig to talk, and had offered to sign the book.

I was both chuffed and disappointed. Chuffed because he clearly liked the images; disappointed because I could not accept the invitation—there were other gigs I had to photograph at the close of this Jazz Fest day, and an opportunity for a photograph wins out over a chance to spend time with an artist—even one you greatly admire (as any good photographer would or should tell you).

CABELL "CAB" CALLOWAY III
25 December, 1907 – 18 November, 1994

I photographed Cab Calloway in Blackpool at the age of 84, two years before he died. I was very conscious of the fact that this would probably be the only chance I would ever get to photograph this great artist—the legendary 'hi-de-ho man', the man responsible for 'Minnie the Moocher' and the leader of one of the most respected pre-World War II big bands with an illustrious alumni that included the likes of Dizzy Gillespie, Doc Cheatham, Ben Webster, Danny Barker and Milt Hilton.

Cab Calloway was also responsible for the hepsters dictionary, a guide to jive language published in 1944. Here's a quick edited A-Z selection:

Armstrongs – musical notes in the upper register, high trumpet notes.

Barbecue – the girl friend, a beauty.

Crumb crushers – teeth.

Dicty – high-class, nifty, smart.

Fine dinner – a good-looking girl.

Gimme some skin – shake hands.

Hincty – conceited, snooty.

Ickaroo – someone who can't dance or dig the jive.

Joint is jumping – the place is lively, the club is leaping with fun.

Killer-diller – a great thrill.

Lay your racket – to jive, to sell an idea, to promote a proposition.

Mitt pounding – applause.

Nix out – to eliminate, get rid of.

Off the cob – corny, out of date.

Piano – Storehouse or Ivories.

Ride – to swing, to keep perfect tempo in playing or singing.

Sky piece – hat.

Togged to the bricks – dressed to kill, from head to toe.

V-8 – a chick who spurns company, is independent, is not amenable.

Wrong riff – the wrong thing said or done.

Xylophone – woodpile.

Yard dog – uncouth, badly attired, unattractive male or female.

Zoot suit – the ultimate in clothes. The only totally and truly American civilian suit.

During a quiet moment in the afternoon sound check back in 1992—when the 'cats were frisking the whiskers'—I approached Cab Calloway. He was leaning on the front of the stage, casting his eye over the setup for his big band's performance later that night.

"Excuse me, Mr. Calloway," I said, trying to catch his attention. He slowly turned his head and caught my gaze with his large sad eyes—they seemed permanently filled with tears. "I just wanted to say hello and let you know that I am a big fan, always have been, and I feel very privileged to be able to see the show and take photographs tonight." He said not a word, and displayed not a reaction. He then slowly turned his head to continue his earlier gaze on the stage. I guess at 84 he was entitled to 'igg' me—he certainly wasn't going to 'beat up the chops' with some 'off the cob' local who hadn't 'got his boots on'.

The show that night was solid and professional, 'in the groove' but not quite 'blowing your wig off'. I remember carefully taking my chance to frame him looking skywards, a single spotlight above his head. He may not have responded to me as I would have hoped earlier, but if this was to be a picture to remember him by, I was going to 'bust my conk' to make it 'righteous'.

All Images: Cab Calloway, Blackpool, 1992

CASSANDRA WILSON
Born 3 December, 1955

Cassandra Wilson is, in my view, the single most important jazz diva to emerge in the last two decades of the twentieth century. There are multiple reasons to single Cassandra Wilson out from many other very fine singers. First there are her singular vocals, like a warm and comforting friend beckoning you to unfamiliar but reassuringly comfortable journeys of the mind, soul and body. *New Yorker* magazine describes her voice as "confidential smokehouse contralto" and the *New York Times* runs with a similar metaphor, "double smoked." I think she is much smoother than that, more like a well-aged boutique whiskey to be shared on special occasions, with special friends.

Secondly, there is her refusal to be constrained by either genre or style, what the New Yorker magazine artfully describes as "wilful originality". Thirdly, there is her reluctance to bask in her star status, making her concerts seem much more like small intimate studio gatherings or a comfortable evening in Cassandra's living room, as she pads barefoot to a lounge chair and sips on a glass of wine (both literally and metaphorically). Fourthly, there is her choice of material which is both eclectic and intriguing. Importantly, her ability to reinterpret jazz, country and pop standards sets her apart as an artist of enduring stature, willing to reach well beyond the comfort zones of any other comparable vocalist of her generation.

Take, for example, her reworking of two classic songs from songbooks not normally considered for inclusion in the repertoire of a jazz singer. 'Last Train to Clarksville' was the Monkees' first hit released back in 1966. At this time the band had just been put together as a television fabrication, and the musicians sang, but did not play, on this first record. Cassandra Wilson reinvents this song with a liltingly beautiful reinterpretation that mines layers of emotions and meaning way beyond the pop affectations of the original. Cassandra brings light and shade to what was once a one-dimensional, disposable pop song. (It is an intriguing footnote to learn that the songwriters, Tommy Boyce and Bobby Hart, now acknowledge that the song was written as an anti-Vietnam protest, but this was kept quiet at the time of the original release to avoid its rejection from commercial television and radio.)

The second example, 'Wichita Lineman' is as quintessentially country as 'Last Train' is pop. This Jimmy Webb song was made famous by Glenn Campbell in 1968, and has since become a staple of the county genre. And yet Cassandra Wilson reinterprets this into a hauntingly simple ballad, and makes this song her own—a true sign, in my book, of a major artist.

For the better part of a decade, I have been an unabridged fan, although in recent years I have noticed an anxiety and preciousness creeping into her concerts. She seems to have lost the warm and cosy living-room feel of her earlier barefoot concerts. This, it must be conceded, might be personal. Cassandra Wilson's management imposed the most draconian conditions on photography I have ever seen in advance of her 2013 performance at the Melbourne International Jazz Festival. This included providing Ms Wilson with the rights to use all photos for any purpose in perpetuity. I politely declined, and so the last photographs I take of Cassandra Wilson might be those from her New Orleans Jazz Festival set of 2008, at which I was publicly admonished. "No photos," she said, singling me out at side stage for attention, "Just Listen!" So I did.

The irony of this exchange was that I was accredited to take photographs and invisible to the audience; the only person concerned about my presence was Cassandra Wilson. Moreover, I have tried to take a definitive photograph of Cassandra Wilson at concerts over the years, but never quite managed to capture the image that would represent the awe and reverence in which I have regarded her. But at this concert, before she took out whatever frustrations she was having that day on me, I captured a series of images I suspected that I would be unlikely to better (just as well, as it turns out). Cassandra, in red, looked stunning and photographed beautifully. Perhaps if she ever sees these photographs, she might just bring herself to think less dismally of the quiet side-stage figure training a lens on her as she performed.

By way of postscript, Cassandra Wilson did permit photography in her 2015 Jazz Fest set, but for just one song. Working as fast as I could, I did manage to capture a few images I was happy with, but continue to be perplexed and frustrated by restrictions which inevitably mean that better images are being missed.

Cassandra Wilson, New Orleans Jazz and Heritage Festival, 2008

Cassandra Wilson, New Orleans Jazz and Heritage Festival, 1996

Top: Cassandra Wilson, TwiRoPa, New Orleans, 2002

Bottom: Cassandra Wilson, New Orleans Jazz and Heritage Festival, 2015

DAVE BRUBECK

6 December, 1920 – 5 December, 2012

Dave Brubeck is one of America's foremost jazz pianists and composers, probably best known for the 1959 hit 'Take Five', which was written by Brubeck's long-time saxophone sideman, Paul Desmond. Written in 5/4 time, it has become an enduring standard, earning substantial royalties which are said to have been donated to the American Red Cross since Desmond's death in 1977. The unusual time signature is consistent with Brubeck's experimentation and exploration of rhythm and structure, harmony and tone.

Over the years his line-ups evolved through jazz quartets, trios (with Gerry Mulligan) and back to quartets and quintets featuring one or more of his sons, four of whom are now professional musicians. He is also an accomplished composer of choral and orchestral pieces, including regular performances with the London Symphony Orchestra. Brubeck remained a prolific performer into his later years, with a range of collaborations and projects that included an orchestral collaboration as an homage to Bach and compositions for the words of the Old Testament, Martin Luther King Jr and the photographs of Ansel Adams.

There are two photographs I have taken of Brubeck that I hope do him justice. Both were taken at London's Royal Festival Hall in the early 1990s. My credentials as David Redfern's nominee (David was a close personal friend of Brubeck) gained me exclusive concert access, but I was required to be very discreet. I managed to get a side-stage photograph which I like to think captures the mood of a working band, and then I quietly made my way to the choir seats upstairs and was attracted to the light and shadow framing Brubeck at his piano.

Brubeck was honored with the National Medal of Arts in 1994, a Grammy Lifetime Achievement Award in 1996 and the Benjamin Franklin Award for Public Diplomacy in 2008. He was inducted into the *DownBeat* jazz magazine Hall of Fame in 1994 and the California Hall of Fame in 2008.

On his 89th birthday, on 9 December 2009, Brubeck's career was honored by the Kennedy Center for his significant contribution to the cultural life of the USA and the world. In the words of the Kennedy Center Chairman, Stephen A. Schwarzman, "Dave Brubeck's genius has dazzled us for six decades and has helped to define an American art form." Speaking at the award presentation at the White House, President Obama recalled a 1971 Brubeck concert in Honolulu, which was the last time Obama had seen his father. "You can't understand America without understanding jazz," Obama said, "and you can't understand jazz without understanding Dave Brubeck."

Below and Right: Dave Brubeck, Royal Festival Hall, London, circa 1992

Doc Cheatham, New Orleans Jazz and Heritage Festival, 1994

DOC CHEATHAM
13 June, 1905 – 2 June, 1997

Doc Cheatham, born Adolphus Anthony Cheatham in Nashville in 1905, performed at the New Orleans Jazz and Heritage Festival in 1994 and 1995. He was warm and generous, and played his trumpet with depth and feeling. He had a style and panache all his own. He made you feel good just to be in the same room. He exuded a zest for life that was infectious and contagious.

This was a man who could draw on 90 years of life experience and a musical career that began with King Oliver and Louis Armstrong, took in Cab Calloway, Billie Holliday and Benny Goodman along the way, and then alighted in New Orleans in 1994 where he passed the baton to 20-year-old Nicholas Payton. In an extraordinary interview at the 1994 New Orleans Jazz and Heritage Festival, he described the young Nicholas Payton as the reincarnation of King Oliver—heady praise indeed from someone who was a devoted acolyte of Oliver back in 1920s Chicago. In 1996 the two trumpeters recorded a CD for Verve Records, *Doc Cheatham and Nicholas Payton*, which won them the 1997 Grammy Award for best jazz instrumental. It was presented posthumously to Doc Cheatham at New York's Radio City Music Hall in February 1998.

Doc Cheatham played his final gig just two days prior to his death at the Blues Alley club in Washington. According to pianist Butch Thompson, his last words to his last audience were: "This is the happiest night of my life."

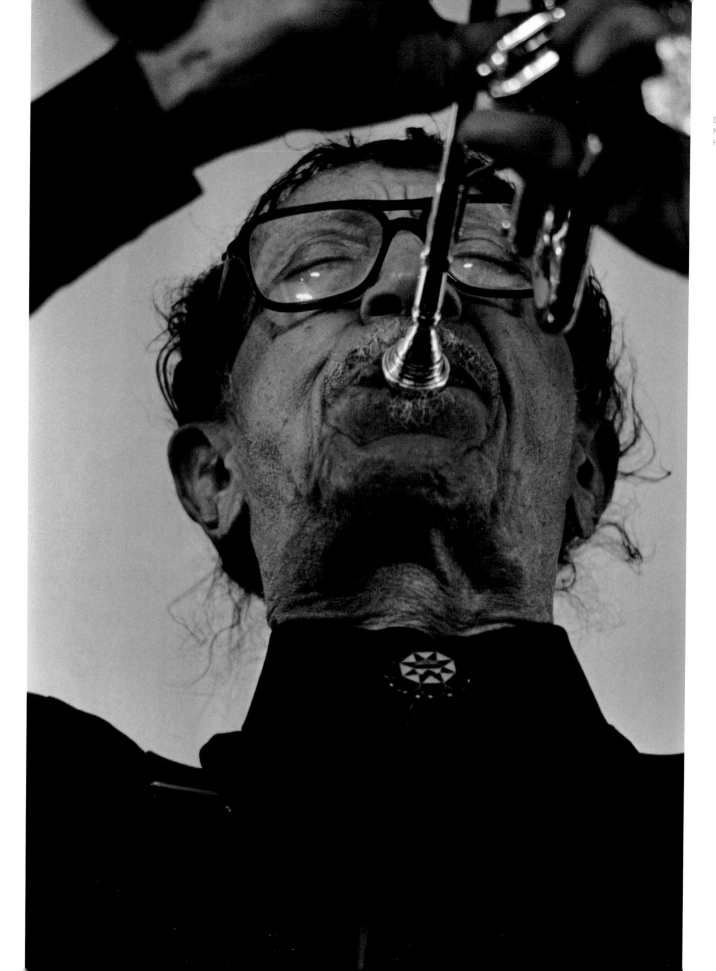

DON PULLEN
25 December, 1941 – 22 April, 1995

Don Pullen was an underrated pianist and composer who suffered for much of his career from ill-informed criticism by traditionalist critics unwilling to embrace the new wave of free and improvised jazz. Pullen, like Ornette Coleman and Eric Dolphy, whom he admired and emulated, was committed to a free form of music performance which was wrongly interpreted at the time as lacking structure. What was missing was not form or structure, but the willingness of listeners to hear a new way of thinking about playing rhythm, melody and harmony. This depended on how the musician felt about the music and how he or she would interact with ensemble players of a like mind.

It wasn't until Pullen began working and recording in Europe in the early 80s that he began to get the level of recognition and acceptance he deserved. The return to the USA of the George Adams/Don Pullen Quartet to record with Blue Note in the second half of the 1980s, however, did not achieve the anticipated home turf success. After the death of drummer Danni Richmond (a fellow Mingus band alumni) in 1988, Pullen recorded his first trio album, *New Beginnings*, with Tony Williams on drums and Gary Peacock on bass. The impact of the album lived up to its name, and Pullen finally received the critical acclaim which had previously eluded him. He is now regarded as a significant artist in his own right and an important co-contributor to the legacy of Charles Mingus, with whom he played and recorded in the first half of the 1970s. Both his simplicity of composition, owing much to the influence of the piano style of Mal Waldron, and his percussive playing style, which featured a unique technique of rolling right hand runs, make Pullen essential listening for any students of the modern jazz idiom.

Pullen would write simple melodies that reminded him of friends and then would weave them into his composition. I don't have a melody that reminds me of Pullen, but I did photograph him rehearsing on stage at the Royal Festival Hall in London in the late 80s. While I don't think he ever saw the images from this session, I think he would have appreciated the simplicity of the light, the piano and his reflection.

Pullen will be remembered as a purist inasmuch as he was committed to what he called a "higher level" of creation. In 1976, he was quoted in an interview in the Canadian magazine *Coda*, "If you play truthful music, it's going to prevail ... so I'll do whatever I have to do to keep it on a high level and get it out to the people ... if I take care of the music, the music will take care of me."

Don Pullen,
Royal Festival Hall, London, circa 1989

MILES DEWEY DAVIS III
26 May, 1926 – 18 September, 1991

If jazz is to become recognized as the new classical music of the twentieth century—as it surely must—then Miles must be acknowledged as one of the pre-eminent figures in that history. Importantly, he will be remembered not only for his talents as a composer, arranger and bandleader, but for his playing. Miles brought a new understanding to the interplay between performance and composition.

My understanding of Miles Davis' contribution to music comes down to three key elements: tone, space and timing. (For an insight into Miles Davis, the man, I recommend his fascinating autobiography.)

Tone refers to the sound of his trumpet—unmistakable, pure and crystal clear; shockingly original when heard for the first time; comfortingly, even achingly familiar, once known and loved. Widely copied, but never bettered (why do so many trumpet players insist on the futile exercise of trying to sound like Miles?), Miles' sound was capable of whispering the deepest spiritual and emotional nuances or proclaiming joy through rhythm and movement.

Space refers to his ability to understand and articulate the importance of silence, and to make room for both the musicians and the audience (whether live or recorded) to feel their way into the music, to be an integral part of the conversation, to not be shouted down or interrupted, to flow and be free, to sit back and absorb. Of all the lessons in my journey into unchartered musical territories, this was the most important—that silence is as important as sound—and nobody articulated this more clearly than Miles. Would that more musicians paid attention.

Timing is a natural and necessary corollary to space, but means more in this context than just the interplay between rhythm and silence. Miles possessed an unerring and uncanny ability to stay ahead of the pack, to lead into new and unchartered areas of musical exploration that could only be named or recognized or understood after Miles had carved them out. In doing this he jettisoned shibboleths of style and broke new ground, often to the chagrin of old or new traditionalists who just couldn't keep up. Miles' pace of change and breadth of sweep was always challenging and confronting. He could just as easily have stood still and milked the deserving accolades, but he chose to move on and take risks—in my view the truest sign of a major and enduring artist.

Miles was sometimes criticized for his penchant to walk off stage or turn his back on the audience during live gigs, but this was, in my experience, missing the point. A live Miles performance was not just about seeing Miles playing trumpet, but rather it was an invitation into the musical world of Miles Davis, and no one could give a more profoundly moving and insightful master class than the man himself—that is, if the listener was prepared to listen, really listen.

I would have dearly cherished the opportunity for a photo session with Miles, and I don't mind acknowledging that there are many images of Miles that are more important than mine. I was lucky enough to photograph Miles on two occasions; the first was at the Hammersmith Odeon in London, around 1985 (I think I was covering the concert for the *NME*). Miles was in rare form, stylishly attired with a tasselled jacket over a kind of up-market grey jump-suit and cowboy boots. A fedora hat and oversized sunglasses—two accessories guaranteed to make the life of a photographer difficult—completed the outfit. He prowled the stage like a lioness in charge of its cubs, restlessly moving on and off the stage, stepping forward to take solos and at one point stopping to pose for an audience member's snap with a compact flash camera.

By chance, I met that audience member some years later in a flat in Kings Cross, London. She was a lifelong fan, absolutely devoted to Miles' *Sketches of Spain* album. The photograph she took that night was a treasured memento—it wouldn't have made the grade for magazine

Miles Davis, New York, circa 1988

reproduction, but it reminded me just how powerful and evocative photographs can be, and how privileged photographers are to document the lives of major artists.

The second time I photographed Miles was in New York at a very unusual gig announced at very short notice. The venue was a mid-town club not known for jazz gigs; if it was known for anything it was for some shady history and rumoured money laundering connections with the mafia. I spent hours and days on the phone trying to hustle my way into the gig, and eventually Miles' manager agreed to meet me outside the gig and bring me in an hour or two before the show was due to start. I turned up as arranged, restlessly pacing the sidewalk as it became increasingly clear that the manager looked like being a no-show. Someone came to the front of the queue to sell a spare ticket just as the doors were being opened. I took my chance, bought the ticket (I think it was something like $50—a lot of money back in those days) and slipped into the club as the doors opened to secure a seat at front of stage right. Once inside, I introduced myself to the manager—he was mildly apologetic about forgetting to get me in and introduced me to a couple of the members of the band.

When Miles came on I started taking photographs in what was very poor light—too low even for the low-light technique I had by then perfected. In those days I was shooting with a Leica M series camera. This was the classic 35mm rangefinder camera that had revolutionized street photography. Importantly, it had the quietest shutter of any camera on the market; it was virtually inaudible. I mention this because I am firmly of the view that photographers need to be cognisant of the impact they can have at concerts, especially jazz performances, where the click of a shutter, or worse still, the sunburst of a flash, can annoy and distract both the performer and the audience. Photographers need to get over their egocentricity; the gig needs to be recorded, yes, but not to the detriment of the artist and the audience.

So here I was at front stage right in a very small and intimate club, enjoying the gig and shooting in a low-key and very quiet manner. Miles became aware of the camera and waved me away—he clearly didn't want me to take photographs. His manager and the drummer noticed this interplay, and they waved me on, motioning to me that I should continue to take photographs. This was seriously weird—in all my years of photographing musicians, I have only been asked to stop taking photographs on two occasions. This was the first occasion, and it was the living artist I most admired. Many years later something similar was to happen with Cassandra Wilson, at the time the living female vocalist I most admired. As my American friends might say, "go figure".

I did persist with taking photographs that night, but even more circumspectly than at the beginning of the concert. Miles seemed to settle down and ignore me after a while, particularly as the gig hotted up and Miles traded licks with a very accomplished keyboard player. At one point Miles conducted what could only be described as a public masterclass with the young bass player—a kind of call and response interplay to coax the bass player down a path Miles wanted to go. This stands out in my memory for three reasons: firstly, I shared my table with a young musician studying the bass in New York; she was absolutely enthralled and it was thrilling to absorb the awe and transferred inspiration. Secondly, I had the sense that Miles was aware of his own place in music history and his own mortality; this was a public lesson in what he had to offer to the next generation of jazz musicians. Thirdly, this interplay afforded me my best photograph of the night: Miles with his head thrown back and tongue poking out. This wasn't an atypical pose, but I'm not sure I've seen another photograph like this. Time will tell whether it was worth persisting with irritating the great Miles Davis after all.

Left and Right Miles Davis, Hammersmith Odeon, London, circa 1985

GIL EVANS
13 May, 1912 – 20 March, 1988

In March 1983, I was commissioned by the *NME* to photograph a live performance by Gil Evans and his orchestra at the Round House in Chalk Farm, London. I was aware that Gil Evans was an important jazz artist with influences that extended through the cool jazz, modern jazz and jazz rock idioms, but I was unaware at the time of the privilege this commission afforded me, and the true stature of the man as a composer, arranger and bandleader.

In some ways I was lucky that a couple of the editors at *NME* —at this time primarily devoted to indie rock and post-punk—understood the significance of Evans and recognized my emerging interest in the genre. The *NME* did not make a habit of covering jazz figures and the period in which I was working for them (early to mid-80s) was also not particularly memorable for indie rock or post-punk. One of those editors went on to co-found Q magazine—but my work with Q lasted only one session (a black and white portrait of Robert Cray), because Q preferred to own the copyright for photographic sessions, and this was not how I chose to work. The other went on to work with *The Face* magazine when it was still setting trends, and I had a lot of fun with a Northern Soul shoot for *The Face* before moving on to more commercial commissions.

The deal with Gil Evans back in 1983 was no photographs during the gig, so I was invited to the sound check. This was quite a normal occurrence back in the 80s—sometimes still is. The plus side is that the photographer gets pretty much open access to the artist and the stage. The downside is that the artist is often not dressed or lit for the stage. Gil was very professional and very focused, and the lighting was adequate, if not ideal. The result was, fortunately, some memorable pictures. Music photography does require both technical skill and a flair for composition, but all the skills and artistic talent in the world mean nothing without access—and that was what I was afforded that day at the Round House.

A couple of years later I went to see Gil Evans and his orchestra at the Sweet Basil on one of my regular visits to New York. Evans had a regular Monday night gig there and his Monday Night Orchestra went on to record several albums, including the Grammy Award-winning *Bud and Bird*, for Best Jazz Instrumental Performance, Big Band in 1989.

There is a very interesting picture of Gil at full stretch conducting his band, photographed side stage through the maze of horns. Sweet Basil was a very small and poorly lit club, but its owner Horst Liepolt was very welcoming, and generous enough to let me hang out at the bar and move forward from time to time to take pictures. Unfortunately that particular negative has gone missing, and all I have of that image is a poor quality work print—and a fond memory.

Luckily the Chalk Farm negatives are safe and the pictures still stand up. The importance of Gil Evans remains undiminished, not the least for his seminal collaborations with Miles Davis on the Miles Ahead album (recorded in the year of my birth, 1957) and *Porgy and Bess* and *Sketches of Spain* in 1958 and 1960 respectively.

Gil Evans, Round House, London, 1983

Gil Evans,
Round House,
London, 1983

Gil Evans,
Sweet Basil,
New York,
circa 1985

JAMES CARTER
Born 3 January, 1969

James Carter is probably the hottest young saxophone player on the jazz scene today. He is an exciting player, capable of considered nuances and blazing runs. He sets the stage alight unlike any other contemporary performer, handling a range of saxophones and clarinet with style, grace and, at times, precocious chutzpah.

His musical pedigree is immaculate—playing and touring with Wynton Marsalis when he was 17 and then joining Lester Bowie's band in New York in 1998. His subsequent collaborations include the late Julius Hemphill, Cyrus Chestnut, Rodney Whitaker, Frank Lowe, Madeleine Peyroux, Ronald Shannon Jackson, the Charles Mingus Big Band, Kathleen Battle, Aretha Franklin, David Murray, Ginger Baker and Sonny Rollins.

He has recorded eighteen albums since his critically acclaimed debut in 1994. In 2000, *Chasin' the Gypsy* demonstrated that musical talent runs strong in the Carter family genes. This album was recorded with his cousin Regina Carter, the remarkably talented and composed young jazz violinist who, among other things, was the first African-American and first jazz musician permitted to play the 1743 Guarnerius violin once owned by Niccolo Paganini.

I have seen James Carter on three occasions in New Orleans, twice as a band leader and once as an unexpected side-man, an occasion that created a ripple of expectation among the knowledgeable crowd. I like the picture of James with the alto because it goes as close to anything I have taken of an artist in capturing the energy and intensity of a live set, and few musicians 'throw down' quite like James Carter.

James took the part of Ben Webster in the 1996 Robert Altman film *Kansas City,* and has effectively monopolized the prestigious *Downbeat* critics poll for the baritone saxophone in recent years. The only question mark hovering over Carter's career and status is just what he may be able to achieve with his extraordinary and prodigious talent.

Right and Below: James Carter, New Orleans Jazz and Heritage Festival, 2007

JIMMY SCOTT
17 July, 1925 – 12 June, 2014

Little Jimmy Scott was the singer's singer, one of the most admired and influential singers of the twentieth century. Sadly, he is also one of several artists who died during the development and production of this book. Scott suffered from a genetic condition, which prevented him reaching puberty and which accounted for both his slight build and his unique contralto voice. It took great courage and a unique talent to overcome the hardships he endured throughout his life.

He first rose to prominence with the Lionel Hampton band in the 1940s, and it was Hampton who gave Scott his moniker, 'Little Jimmy Scott'. What Scott did with his voice was all about heart and interpretation. No one could sit behind the beat like Jimmy Scott, extracting every last drop of soul and emotion from a song, and then some. He truly was an amazing vocalist and an extraordinarily powerful and emotive performer. He carried with him a captivating and unrivalled emotional intensity, his delicate hand movements twisting to the pain or joy or suffering he made almost physical with his exquisite voice.

He had a legion of admirers from Billie Holiday and Dinah Washington through to Marvin Gaye and Elton John. Ray Charles signed him to his label in 1962 and described Scott as "singing soul way back before the word was being used." Lou Reed said he has "the voice of an angel and can break your heart" and Madonna is said to have told a journalist that Scott is the only singer that can make her cry. He is also probably the only artist to have sung the same song at the inaugurations of two presidents forty years apart. In 1943 and 1993 he sang 'Why Was I Born' for Eisenhower and Clinton respectively, with each inauguration roughly coinciding with his early and later golden periods.

I only saw Scott once, at Jazz Fest in 2001, but it was more than enough to make me a true believer and immediately go out and purchase his CDs, something I reserve for just a few artists each year. He continued to tour to a devoted fan base, particularly in Europe and Japan, into his later years. A one-of-a-kind, it is hard to imagine how his unique musical gift could ever be replicated.

Right and Below: Little Jimmy Scott, New Orleans Jazz and Heritage Festival, 2001

MAX ROACH
10 January, 1924 – 16 August, 2007

Max Roach was one of the most important innovators in the development of modern jazz. He was far and away the most exciting and inspiring drummer I have ever seen perform live.

In the 1940s, Roach and Kenny Clarke ushered in the bebop era, revolutionizing the role and style of drumming forever. By using the cymbal rather than the bass drum to keep the time signature, Clarke and Roach opened up the full potential of the drum kit, allowing room for the drummer to improvise and explore the links between rhythm and melody. In effect Roach helped liberate the drummer, and he took full advantage of this license throughout his career, exploring all manner of collaborations and opportunities both in jazz and beyond.

Roach's jazz collaborations read like a *Who's Who* of the bebop and avant-garde jazz world. He was there when Charlie Parker recorded his seminal bebop recordings in 1947 and 1948, and when Miles Davis recorded *Birth of the Cool* in 1949. He worked, among others, with Charles Mingus, Coleman Hawkins, Dizzy Gillespie, Duke Ellington, Bud Powell, George Coleman, Sonny Rollins, Clifford Brown, Cecil Taylor, Anthony Braxton, Archie Shepp, Abdullah Ibrahim, Mal Waldron and Clark Terry.

In his later years he continued to evolve, playing in his percussion-only ensemble, M'boom, and performing in a range of settings: solo, duets, quartets and double quartets (with string quartets added). He won a *Village Voice* magazine Obie award for his music written for three Sam Shepard plays in 1995, collaborated with multimedia artists and continued his ground-breaking collaborations with the African-American modern dance master, Alvin Ailey, until Ailey died in 1989. Roach was also a key figure in legitimising and identifying the links between hip hop and jazz.

Always the innovator, always pushing boundaries, Roach rejected any criticism levelled at his collaborations with avant-garde artists like Archie Shepp, Cecil Taylor and Anthony Braxton. Roach saw new and progressive musical experimentation as building on the foundations of an evolving jazz history. Roach knew and understood that innovators like Charlie Parker would not have expected their music to stand still. Subsequent generations of musicians would stay true to the art form not by imitating their predecessors, but by boldly taking risks in new endeavors that might succeed or fail.

This role, as the last living ambassador of innovation from the group of musicians that changed music forever back in the 1940s, is a critically important legacy for the future of this art form. Roach is quoted in an article by Mike Zwerin in January 1999 (http://www.culturekiosque.com/jazz/miles/rhemile29.htm): "And then there are people who push forward, who perpetuate the continuum by trying out things. Cecil Taylor is more like Art Tatum than a guy who plays like Tatum. It may not always come off, but that's what creativity's about."

I first saw Max Roach in a New York club in the late 80s. I will never forget the electric energy that night, and my realisation for the first time that a home turf gig is unlike any other. It seemed as if most of the audience knew Roach personally, and senior figures in the jazz world were on hand to push Roach to perform way above par. In retrospect it was probably this gig that initiated my lifelong preference for live jazz performance over recordings.

In concerts in his later years, Roach would pare his kit back to the high hat and snare; this was all he needed for an exhilarating solo exploration of the potential of the drums. My abiding memory of Max Roach is being wrapped up in his warmth and generosity of spirit, totally lost and enthralled as he sat upright and beaming, demonstrating his encyclopaedic depth of knowledge and reference points, and his extraordinary musical prowess.

Left:
Max Roach,
New Orleans Jazz and
Heritage Festival, 2001

Right:
Max Roach,
New York, circa 1988

NINA SIMONE
21 February, 1933 – 21 April, 2003

Born Eunice Kathleen Waymon in Tryon, North Carolina, Nina Simone was nothing less than the most singular and exceptional talent I have ever seen. Her official website describes her as a singer, pianist, arranger and composer, honorary doctor in music and humanities, 'high priestess of soul" and "Queen of African Rooted Classical Music." I saw Nina perform on three separate occasions, and at each performance she more than lived up to each of these descriptions, avoiding any outbursts of temperament for which she was also famous.

The first concert I saw her perform was in the mid to late 80s, fittingly at Ronnie Scotts' club in Soho, London. Ronnie Scotts holds a unique place in jazz folklore and in the musical history of Nina Simone in particular. A live recording from 1984, released in 1987, helped rekindle her career after a self-imposed exile from the USA. Her popularity took off when her original 1958 recording of 'My Baby Just Cares for Me' became a major hit in 1987 following its use in a television advertisement for the perfume Chanel No 5. On the back of this, Nina deservedly remained an A-list performer for the rest of her life. Ronnie Scotts was also known as Nina's venue of choice for no-shows or early departures—at previous residencies she was known to either storm off stage early or not turn up at all—but these are stories for others to tell, because I was not there.

The Ronnie Scotts gig I saw had Nina on song, both for her vocals and for her piano playing, which was often underrated, such was the power and dominance of that unique voice. The gig I saw could not have been filmed because the lighting was terrible (as it usually was at Ronnie's). On this night, a single white spotlight barely traced out her profile at side stage left. There were no useable photographs that night, but fortunately my best opportunity to photograph Nina was still to come.

The second time I saw Nina was at the first (and last) Blackpool Jazz Festival in 1992. Whichever way you looked at it, Blackpool was not a prestigious music venue and the organisers were very, very nervous; they were keenly aware of Nina's chequered performance history and were doing everything they could to smooth the path. Nina turned up for the afternoon sound check in a grumpy mood; she was unhappy about the position of the piano on the stage and very annoyed that there was no fan at the side of the piano.

Those two matters settled, she proceeded through the paces of the sound check and then, for no apparent reason, shifted mood. The spirit of the music and the joy of the woman took over. By this stage of the sound check, her entire audience consisted of two disinterested technicians and one enthralled photographer (camera at rest). Nina shimmied to the front of the stage, jiving and gyrating her sassy way through her rendition of the folk song, See-Line Woman:

Nina Simone, Blackpool, 1992

See-Line Woman, she drink coffee,
she drink tea, then she go home

See-Line Woman, dressed in white,
sleep all day, ball all night

See-Line Woman, dressed in green,
wear silk stockings, golden seams

See-Line Woman, dressed in yella,
watch out girls, she gonna steal your fella

See Line Woman, dressed in brown,
watch out fellas, she gonna get down

See-Line Woman, dressed in black,
sleep all day, on her back

See-Line Woman, dressed in red,
wear a rag on her head

Wiggle wiggle, purr like a cat,
wink at a man, then he wink back

Empty his pockets, wreck his days,
make him love her, then she sure fly away.

Wow! Words escape me even these many years later. I rate this as the most privileged moment of my life in music. Tongue in cheek, I sometimes call this the time Nina performed for me alone, but in truth, she performed for Nina, and Nina alone. I was just lucky, very lucky, to be there.

I remember very little of that night's concert, awash as I was in the glow of the afternoon's performance. The photographs, however, speak for themselves; Nina was strong, powerful, assured and in control that night, but nothing could compare to those few minutes earlier in the day.

The next time I saw Nina was in a large meeting hall in Brixton in south London. I don't think I knew exactly where the meeting was, what it was about, or who organised it when I stepped off the Northern Line tube train at Brixton station, but I did know Nina was going to be there. It turned out to be an extraordinary acclamation of Nina as a role model for independent black women, this at a time when racial and sexual politics in England were highly contested and unresolved, but when many young second-generation British-born blacks were beginning to carve out their own identities in the cultural melting pot that was London in the eighties.

I never saw Nina again, but she remains, in my view, incomparable—my favorite female vocalist of all time. When she died, what else could I do but spit out the words that she had first recorded back in 1964 at the height of the civil rights movement: "Mississippi Goddam."

Nina Simone, Brixton, London, circa 1993

Ornette Coleman,
New Orleans Jazz and Heritage Festival, 2003

ORNETTE COLEMAN
Born 9 March, 1930

Ornette Coleman is one of the great free-thinkers and innovators of jazz in the post-bebop period. His official website says, "His revolutionary musical ideas have been controversial, but today his enormous contribution to modern music is recognized throughout the world."

Coleman was at the forefront of a new era of free jazz. With his early avant-garde recordings, the aptly titled *Something Else, The Shape of Jazz to Come,* and *Free Jazz: A Collective Improvisation* released in 1958, 1959 and 1960 respectively, Coleman polarised listeners into ardent fans or unbelievers. His music flirted with dissonance and jarred with preconceived notions about melody and harmony. What many of the naysayers were not yet hearing were the 'Harmolodics' at the center of this tumult. This new musical philosophy was deliberately and intentionally challenging, and I confess that I came to Ornette Coleman very late in his career, and more than a little wary of his reputation for inaccessibility.

The London concert I first saw Coleman perform at in the early 1990s dispelled all notions of discomfort and concern I might previously have felt. I found Coleman's music heartfelt, moving and accessible. I found it both melodic and harmonic. I immediately warmed to this gentle and humble man at the center of this aural experience.

I now understood that the critical discourse that had gone before was an unnecessary distraction and diversion. 'Harmolodics' does not eschew rhythm and harmony and melody and fine musicianship, it simply strips away preconceptions about what is important within the various elements of a composition and how it should be played. These decisions are left to the performers. But as Coleman points out in his manifesto published on his website:

> You really have to have players with you who will allow your instincts to flourish in such a way that they will make the same order as if you [had] sat down and written a piece of music. To me, that is the most glorified goal of the improvising quality of playing—to be able to do that.

Ornette Coleman may be an intellectual and a deep thinker in his radical approach to music, but he is not didactic, nor is his philosophy difficult to unravel. There is always a rhythm–melody–harmony concept. All ideas have lead resolutions.

> Each player can choose any of the connections from the composer's work for their personal expression. ... In music, the only thing that matters is whether you feel it or not.

In many ways, Coleman's philosophy is, by definition, infinitely accessible. The music is in the hands of the players, the reception is in the mind of the listener. As he said, "Harmolodics is not a style. Those who judge the concept of Harmolodic playing are using outdated terms to describe their knowledge. All listeners are equal in their opinions."

Live on stage, Coleman gets caught deep inside what he is playing. When he surfaces from this intense exploration, to acknowledge the applause of the audience, for example, it is as if he finds himself embarrassed to be in the spotlight. He appears more like a diffident child on his first day at school than a musical revolutionary. He is humble and unassuming, a personal trait that endears the listener even more to the man and his music. I think this is why I like the simple portrait of Ornette Coleman from 2003; for me it captures that awkward interstitial moment when Coleman must acknowledge his relationship with the crowd, before diving back into the safety and security of his musical world.

Ornette Coleman's accolades have arrived late, but confirm that his visionary approach to music is now finally well and truly anchored in this new mainstream of jazz discourse. He was the second jazz artist to win a Pulitzer Prize, for his album *Sound Grammar,* in 2006. In 2007 he received a Grammy Award for Lifetime Achievement and in 2008 he was inducted into the Neshui Ertegun Jazz Hall of Fame at New York's Jazz at Lincoln Center. In 2009 he received the Miles Davis Award from the Festival Internationale de Montréal.

One of my favorite quotes from Coleman's Harmolodics manifesto is a credo that should apply to all creative endeavors in life (including the writing and editing of this book): "It was when I realized I could make mistakes that I decided I was really on to something."

Top and Bottom: Ornette Coleman, London, circa 1992

SONNY ROLLINS

7 September, 1930

Theodore Walter Rollins, born in New York in 1930, knew from his youth that he would be devoting his life to the pursuit of art and spirituality through the medium of a saxophone. It was just the way it was always going to be.

He grew up in Harlem, around the corner from The Savoy Ballroom and the Apollo Theatre, in the same neighborhood as his saxophone idol, Coleman Hawkins. Inspired by the music of early innovators like Fats Waller and Louis Armstrong, he originally took up alto saxophone, but switched to tenor as a teenager to emulate Hawkins.

His rise to prominence as a creative force in jazz was meteoric. In the 1950s, still only in his twenties, he produced some of his most enduring work, fronting groups that included luminaries like Miles Davis, Thelonious Monk and Max Roach, and recording the album *Saxophone Colossus* in 1956, which included compositions like 'St. Thomas', which has become a jazz standard.

Sonny however, thought he could do better. At the height of his fame, around 1959, he disappeared from the jazz scene in Harlem and 52nd Street for a two-year self-imposed sabbatical. Rather than disturb the new-born baby in his neighboring apartment on Grant Street in the Lower East Side, he would climb to the walkway of the Williamsburg Bridge, 135 feet above the East River, and play to the bridge, the river, the sky and the city. His comeback album, in 1962, was aptly titled *The Bridge*.

I wasn't around in those heady days

Sonny Rollins, Melbourne, 2011

teaching an ecstatic audience how to swing, how to move, and how to lose yourself in the joy of sound.

A few weeks later, this time in a cold and wintry Melbourne theatre, a world away from the hot and steamy New Orleans jazz stage, Rollins was rugged up in a scarf and beanie as he explained his philosophy of life, music and art to an audience of admirers. "Improvising is the supreme expression. You are creating something new every time you go on stage—this is the highest form of creative expression."

This idea of jazz as the highest art form is a recurring theme in interviews Rollins gave throughout his career. Rollins says he cannot play the same thing twice. For Rollins, playing music is like meditation. When he is playing, he tries to clear his mind and let the music transcend life and death. He is invoking a journey through which he conjures the spirits of all the greats he has worked with in the past, and has now come to represent. Artists such as Clifford Brown, Coleman Hawkins, Bud Powell, Thelonious Monk, Jackie Maclean, Miles Davis, Max Roach, Don Cherry—the list goes on.

When he was awarded the prestigious Polar Prize from the King of Sweden in Stockholm in 2007, he was described as the greatest remaining master from one of jazz's seminal eras, and one of the most powerful and personal voices in jazz for more than 50 years. "Sonny Rollins has elevated the unaccompanied solo to the highest artistic level—all characterised by a distinctive and powerful sound, irresistible swing

when his reputation as an exciting young tenor swept him to fame, but I have been fortunate enough to see him perform as a venerated elder of jazz at two Jazz Fests: first in 1995 and then in 2011. Shortly after the 2011 performance—perhaps one of the greatest tour de forces I have ever witnessed—I was privileged to hear him speak in an interview series as part of the 2011 Melbourne International Jazz Festival.

Superlatives simply don't do justice to the intensity and joy of the 2011 performance in the jazz tent at New Orleans. This is a venue that regularly sees memorable performances, but this was a concert for the ages, and Rollins knew it: he was on top form and was moving like a youngster, punching the air during his solos and finding intoxicating rhythmic grooves and patterns that drew on a lifetime of musical explorations referencing Africa, New York, New Orleans and the Caribbean. You really had to be there, and all those that were will never forget the experience of this old man, this survivor of the evolution of modern jazz, leading and

and an individual musical sense of humor." In the 2009 video, 'Sonny Rollins—It's All Good', Rollins describes his music as a force of nature. "It's a feeling, a sense of liberation, a sense of communing with nature, with higher things, an abandonment of spirit, a sense of hope, a sense of happiness—that's some of what jazz is."

In Melbourne, in 2011, Rollins explained that he has had many transcendental experiences working with the giants of modern jazz. "You have to have an ego as a performer," he says, "but you have to keep it under control." A young woman—young enough to be his granddaughter, or perhaps even his great-granddaughter—asks him how he would feel if someone was to put lyrics to his music, and sing. He considers this for a while—it's an unusual question, one he probably hasn't been asked before—and then he replies in this languid way he has of talking. Each syllable is individually elongated and enunciated. He knows exactly what he wants to say: "E—la—ted."

SUN RA

22 May, 1914 – 30 May, 1993

There will probably never be another Sun Ra, or anyone quite like Sun Ra. To say he was from another planet is to take literally his story that he was teleported to Saturn and told to speak to the world through music by alien creatures with antennae on their eyes and ears.

Born Herman Poole Blount in Birmingham, Alabama on May 22, 1914, it wasn't until October 20, 1952 that he legally changed his name to Le Sony'r Ra. In what can be considered an artistic statement of political intent, he completely rejected what he called his former slave name and adopted a new persona uniquely suited to the composer and band leader he became.

His music always pushed the boundaries of the jazz and classical forms he drew upon, and his inventive use of keyboards and electronic synthesisers was uniquely suited to his explorations of cosmic jazz, conducted free jazz (which he once described as music of the sun) and the modern or avant-garde jazz canon. Sun Ra's music and composition was ahead of its time, a sort of self-contained and carefully managed improvisational universe of his and Arkestra's own making. His collaboration with long-time Arkestra members such as Marshall Allen and John Gilmore was clearly pivotal to the process and the performance, and Marshall Allen now leads the band on international tours and performances.

I only saw Sun Ra once, in a basement concert in the Village Vanguard around 1988, but I have seen his trumpeter Michael Ray on a few occasions since, and I also saw the full Arkestra on tour in Melbourne in 2011. I remember being completely bemused by the New York show—I couldn't quite understand what the band was trying to achieve, but I was enthralled by the show and pleased to have had just enough light to get a halfway decent exposure of Sun Ra.

What I have come to think since is this: Sun Ra and his Arkestra had enormous improvisational talent. They were fine musicians who understood rhythm and improvisation, and how to work with each other within that framework. Their music is not impenetrable, nor is it discordant. It is rhythmically alive, compositionally intriguing, often challenging, but mostly, and above all, it swings.

An Arkestra concert is enjoyable and should be taken no more seriously than any other composition or improvised work. I suspect Sun Ra was a way-out character with a way-out sense of humor and a way-out way of talking, thinking and philosophising. This probably means you can dip in and out of what he did or says, or take it as seriously or irreverently as your interest or context permits.

Sun Ra certainly understood the value of innovation, collaboration, improvisation and spectacle. It should come as no surprise that George Clinton is a big fan. P-Funk, Clinton's rambling collective of musicians and performers, held together by a ubiquitous funk groove, seems to me to be just a latter-day, funked-up version of the Arkestra. If I am right, then that alone is a worthwhile legacy.

Sun Ra, Village Gate, New York, circa 1988

Jimmy Heath, New Orleans Jazz and Heritage Festival, 2002

Left Top to Bottom:
Gato Barbieri, New York, 2009
Al Jarreau, New Orleans Jazz and Heritage Festival, 2003
Wayne Shorter, New Orleans Jazz and Heritage Festival, 2010
Horace Silver, New Orleans Jazz and Heritage Festival, 1994

Slim Gaillard, Wag Club, London, circa 1988

Right Top to Bottom:
Abdullah Ibrahim, south London rehearsal, circa 1988
Abbey Lincoln, New Orleans Jazz and Heritage Festival, 2002
Mal Waldron, Jazz Café, London, circa 1992
Grover Washington, Blackpool, 1992

McCoy Tyner,
New Orleans Jazz and
Heritage Festival, 2005

Herbie Hancock,
New Orleans Jazz and
Heritage Festival, 2012

Archie Shepp,
New Orleans Jazz and
Heritage Festival, 1995

Dee Dee Bridgewater, New Orleans Jazz and Heritage Festival, 2010

Chick Corea, New Orleans Jazz and Heritage Festival, 2014

Regina Carter, New Orleans Jazz and Heritage Festival, 2012

Dr. Lonnie Smith, New Orleans Jazz and Heritage Festival, 2007

Diana Krall, New Orleans Jazz and Heritage Festival, 2000

Roy Hargrove, New Orleans Jazz and Heritage Festival, 2007

Jamie Cullum, New Orleans Jazz and Heritage Festival, 2005

Frank Morgan, New Orleans Jazz and Heritage Festival, 2001

Charles Lloyd, New Orleans Jazz and Heritage Festival, 2015

Dianne Reeves, New Orleans Jazz and Heritage Festival, 2015

BLUES

REBIRTH OF THE BLUES

First published in the Good Weekend *Magazine*
(The Sydney Morning Herald *and* The Age), *12 October 1996*

Earlier this year, the remnants of the wooden shack in which bluesman Muddy Waters once lived were removed, log by log, from the Stovall Plantation in Coahoma County, Mississippi. The spot is just a short drive from the crossroads of highways 49 and 61, where legend has it Robert Johnson sold his soul to the devil in exchange for his blues guitar skills. After careful restoration, the shack will begin a five-year promotional tour around the fast-growing American chain of music theme clubs The House of Blues, before being returned to its original site.

The crossroads of highways 49 and 61 mark the entrance to the town of Clarksdale, signposting the town's reputation as the home of the blues. But Clarksdale itself has been slow to cotton on. About 18 months ago, the head of Clarksdale's local tourism authority snarled at a northern interloper with plans to turn Clarksdale's disused railway station into a blues tourism attraction. "What makes you think that people are going to pay to see a black man play the guitar?" Now, however, the county tourism authority has received a Federal government grant to renovate the station and the interloper holds the exclusive liquor licence for a performance, tourism and shopping theme complex to be called Bluesland. The blues, it seems, has come a long way.

The small number of (mostly) men who brought Mississippi blues from its Deep South origins were the descendants of African slaves whose freedom was illusory. Their musical response to the hardship and attention of exploitative sharecropping and overt, institutional racism had largely been ignored, until a resurgence of interest in the blues was triggered by the British invasion of rock musicians, notably the Stones, in the '60s.

In hindsight it is difficult to exaggerate the impact the blues has had on contemporary culture. Quite simply, without the blues there would be no rock 'n' roll. Jim Dickinson, a white, Memphis-based musician who participated in what he calls "cultural collision" between black and white music-makers in the '50s and '60s that created what we now know as rockabilly, soul and rock, challenges us to "imagine the world without rock 'n' roll." One of Clarksdale's leading contemporary blues musicians, Arthneice Jones, simply says, "The blues had a baby and they called it rock 'n' roll." In the words of Robert Gordon, a writer and maker of films on Memphis music, rock 'n' roll is simply "the failed attempt of white people with a country background trying to play the blues."

Dickinson traces a neat musical history back to the African origins of slavery.

> An African work song is not a complaint—it is a celebration of life. Add to that slavery the four beat of Anglo Saxon ballad form, and it becomes a complaint of the human condition—it's the blues. You take that back across the line to a teenage white kid who puts a four beat at the bottom of it, and it's rock 'n' roll.

Clarksdale, Mississippi is an obvious starting point in trying to understand the blues—where it came from and what it means today. Clarksdale is in the heartland of what is known as the Mississippi Delta. Not a delta at all, it is, in fact, the floodplains of the mighty Mississippi River—the richest farming land in the United States. The Delta is said to run from the lobby of the Peabody Hotel in Memphis south to Vicksburg, where the American Civil War was won and lost. It is about two hundred miles long and seventy miles wide, bounded to the east by the hill country around Greenwood and to the west by the Yazoo River, which snakes south to Vicksburg.

Driving into the Delta from any direction is like stepping backwards into a world strangely familiar from the documentary and news footage of the American civil rights movement. The grey and dusty furrows of the cotton fields that stretch in every direction speak to the desolation and despair of rural poverty—a reminder of slavery and sharecropping in the not-too-distant past. The promise of cotton abloom on these same fields speaks of the life of plenty on the 'other side of the tracks', where suburban and rural mansions boast their wealth, seemingly oblivious to the neighbouring poverty. Tragically, rural hardship now meets the symptoms of urban disaffection: crime, crack use and teenage pregnancies are on the rise.

Arthneice Jones knows what it is like to live on the wrong side of the tracks. He lives on a Clarksdale street that is broken by a derelict railway line. To drive from the town side of the street to the side on which Jones lives requires a detour of at least six blocks.

The railway line that marks this separation is the same railway line that carried Muddy Waters north to Chicago in 1943. It is the same railway line that carried hundreds of thousands of southern blacks north after World War I—a desperate bid to escape the racism of the Deep South—in the single largest internal migration of people in American history.

Jones represents a generation of bluesmen indebted to their blues ancestors but doing what blues has always done—moved with the times. He is just as likely to be cooking up a party with driving soul music as reaching down into the depths of the blues tradition to experiment with links to jazz and rap. This is how he describes the origin of the blues:

> The black people brought forth the blues through being suppressed; through hard times and denial; through being hated, not loved; through being misunderstood as another race in another world where you once were bought and sold. And the same act went on and on for hundreds of years past the time of slavery. They still took advantage of people. We was just a denied people, as we are today.

James "Super Chikan" Johnson, Clarksdale, 1996

The blues, according to Jones, was

the feeling of expression, to be able to talk back, to speak in another way in a language on our side of town. To blow off steam when you [white people] weren't there. You wasn't going to listen to that nigger music—no way. But it was a form of art being developed right around you for years and years and years that controlled the basic front part of the beat of modern music.

African slaves were first brought to America in 1619. It wasn't until 1862 that the first of a series of constitutional amendments began the process of abolishing slavery. By 1870, slavery was unconstitutional but the misery of southern blacks continued through a cruel and exploitative sharecropping system. Black labourers would farm land and 'share' profits with the landowner. The landowner would deduct expenses from the sharecroppers' half so that most black workers earned a pittance or, worse, built up debts to landlords who built plantation houses of overwhelming grandeur.

For the black workers and their families, the enduring 'shotgun' shack—so named because a bullet fired from the front door would pass straight through the simple two-room shack and out the back door—has come to represent their life of hardship and violent oppression. These days, the ubiquitous trailer home is slowly replacing the shotgun shack as the main housing for the rural poor.

It is in one of these leaking and rickety trailer homes in a desolate trailer park that Jessie Mae Hemphill, one of the great female blues musicians, now languishes. Jessie Mae Hemphill is the last of the Hemphill blues family. Taught by her grandfather, Sid—one of the legendary greats from the hill country marking the eastern border of the Delta—she came to blues performance late in life but has won three major blues awards for the one album she recorded, She-Wolf. She recently suffered a stroke at the age of 60 and is partly paralysed. Most of her possessions were stolen when she was hospitalised with the stroke.

Hemphill's single album and the occasional song on an anthology is all that is left of her legacy to the blues. "I'm staying on God's side now," she says. If she records or performs again, it will be in the gospel tradition.

The tension between the blues and the church is a continuing theme in the Deep South. These days the description of the blues as the Devil's music is more directed towards the lifestyle associated with it than the music itself.

The Reverend Willie Morganfield is an accomplished gospel singer with 13 records to his name. He fondly remembers his cousin, McKinley Morganfield (the legendary Muddy Waters), playing blues on a keg of nails. "There's a thin line between love and hate, same thing with blues and gospel," he says.

Of the Mississippi musicians I spoke to, all of the older musicians and many of the younger ones spoke of their faith in the church as their spiritual guide in the face of hardship and oppression. Of the four old-timers I tracked down, each had stories of physical torment in the cotton fields, and all spoke of the stringent discipline—"whuppings"—that characterised parental and penal discipline in their younger years.

In 1900, W.E.B. Du Bois, one of the early leaders of the black civil rights movement talked of the color line in southern America. "A line drawn in black and white and the blood red of violence." Between 1900 and 1930, the 17 counties of the Mississippi Delta averaged a lynching every five-and-a-half months. Of the 539 recorded lynchings in the US between 1882 and 1964, more than one-third occurred in Mississippi.

Willie Foster grew up through these times. At 75, he is the living embodiment of the original blues man. Still playing the warm and soulful harmonica that made him one of Muddy Waters' favorite side-men, he is now almost blind and is confined to a wheelchair. Foster explains the origins of the blues like this:

I wasn't a slave, my parents weren't, but my fore-fore-parents were. We were writing the same book that the slaves were; they just didn't name it slavery. The only thing was you was not bought. I saw enough of it to know.

Foster certainly does know. As he puts it,

I was born in the blues and raised in the blues. I've had all kind of blues from the broken-toenail blues to the last-strand-of-hair-in-my-head blues. As low as I am and tall as I am. In other words, I've had the hungry blues, the hurtin' blues, the hard-workin' blues, the couldn't-go-to-school blues.

Despite a tragic personal history, he maintains a warmth and joy that defies his life story. He personifies the words that introduce the Civil Rights Museum, built around the hotel in Memphis where Martin Luther King, Jr. was assassinated. "The history of African-Americans in this country is one of tragedy and violence, but it is also one of courage and strength, filled with determination and hope."

In 1921, Foster was born while his mother was working in a cotton field. Tears flow from this blind man's eyes as he recollects the memory of his childhood nearly 70 years before.

I knew what the blues was when I was seven years old. I didn't have anyone to play with and I decided to ask my Mama why don't she get me a sister or brother? That's when I realised what the blues was all about. She said enough to let me know that I was the causing of it. I was born out across the field and they didn't have time to rush me in and cut my navel string, so it kind of mortified. About six months later, my mother's health began to get bad and she couldn't have any more children . . .

Foster, like most of the old-timers still alive today, knows what it was to work from sun-up to sun-down ploughing rock-hard ground with mule teams that would be worked to death in the stinking heat of the cotton fields. "Music," he says, "is a thing beginning from a hoe. You chop

Arthneice Jones, at home, Clarksdale, 1996

the grass and it goes *ching ching*. A man be cutting wood and he go ting ting as he hit the wood and his axe is saying *pop pop pop*. That's a musical sound."

"The name blues," he explains, "is from 'I'm blue'. We put the "ues" to it when you feelin' down and out. You feel sad and blue and hurting. That puts a burden on your mind and makes you feel blue. The blues is an inspiration to keep you from crying because you're tired."

A few miles away, in the center of Greenville, lives Eugene Powell, one of the last great blue guitar pickers. "The blues," he says, "comes from colored people. Colored peoples wasn't counted with white folk. Nobody seemed to like colored people—do them bad, beat 'em up. The blues is playing your feelings." In his song 'Suitcase Full of Trouble', Powell sings:

> *I've got a suitcase full of trouble and a trunk full of worries.*
> *Blues ain't nothin' but a worry on my mind.*
> *You be bothered all the time.*

Foster, Powell and a handful of other old-timers are all that is left of today's advertising stereotype. The old man playing guitar or harmonica on the front porch is not the same as today's blues men and women because the problems are not the same. As Arthneice Jones explains:

> B.B. King can go in through the front door now. When he first started travelling he had to go in the back door. He can drink out of any water fountain now. You'd have had a colored water fountain and a white water fountain. Music has to be about what goes on in your life. New blues is just new problems.

Jones the poet and songwriter takes over:

> *All the cotton been picked and the mules been ploughed,*
> *The story been told and laid to the side.*
> *A lot of folks have written about the blues*
> *But most of them have lied.*
> *In order to know the truth you must have lived the life and damn near died.*

John Ruskey is curator at the Delta Blues Museum in Clarksdale, Mississippi. A musician himself with the Wesley Jefferson Blues Band, he greets thousands of visitors from all parts of the globe coming to Clarksdale to learn and pay their respects to the greats and the music they love. Ruskey argues that the only way to understand the blues is through its performance. "People dance and actively participate in the making of the music. There's a lot of call back and forth between the musicians and audience. It's kind of a communal moving on—that's the hope of the music." Ruskey says,

> Music is a way of telling your story, of talking to people, telling your feelings. Music is an integral part of life here and is as important as talking is to an English teacher or a computer to a Wall Street banker. Music is found at all weddings, family reunions, community gatherings and the juke joints, in the church with gospel music, riding around in your car, in your home.

Live music performance in the Delta is usually confined to Friday or Saturday nights, with the juke joint tradition living on. The juke joint is usually a run-down building that comes alive as a bar and music venue on weekends. The most regular juke joints are in Clarksdale and nearby Shelby. The musicians of this region are a close-knit family and play together at juke joints, clubs and on special occasions.

I was fortunate enough to be invited to several of these gigs, and a description of just two may help to explain what the blues means as a living, rather than a recorded, tradition.

The opening night of a new club in Clarksdale attracted most local musicians to perform and jam together. Special guest was Terry "Youngblood" Williams, who had been released from the local jail for the evening to play for the first time in three months.

Williams had been jailed for failing to make fine payments on a minor drug charge. He had been arrested by his parole officer when he came off stage from the 1995 Annual Sunflower Festival in Clarksdale. The last time he had picked up a guitar was in February 1996 when he

was released to pay at a benefit concert. Referring to his time in jail, Williams told me, "Since I've been I here I've been divorced. I've been spit on, slapped on. Well, I know what the blues is all about now."

Williams plays with a sweetness of sound and deftness of touch that belies his recent experience and underscores the talent of real blues men. When he was joined by his two young sons, the soul of the blues man was poignant. His skill lies in a confidence in his own ability and musical heritage not to show off with the loud and showy licks that characterise many white blues players. Just as jazz music is largely about knowing when not to play, real blues is all about feeling and expression, and fine blues musicians can create more feeling and sensitivity with one bent note than the flashy affectations of rock musicians and their desperate attempts to demonstrate their arsenal of guitar skills.

Later that same night, thirty miles away in the town of Shelby, Robert Walker was playing at the region's most active juke joint, the Do Drop Inn. A cotton grower from Mississippi now growing cotton in California, Walker had returned to Shelby for a family funeral. The Do Drop Inn is a crumbling façade on a rundown corner. On weekends the streets are alive with people and cars. A couple of dollars at the door gains entrance to a long rectangular room with large sheets of chipboard covering the floors, walls and low ceiling. In the front half of the room is a bar and pool table, while there is a seating, dance and performance area in the back half of the room.

Walker plays with an intensity that can only be compared to Chuck Berry at his dirtiest. Backed by the irrepressible James "Super Chikan" Johnson on drums and a languid bass player holding down the beat, Walker's playing inspired extraordinary audience reaction, from licentious dancing through to respectful homage and interplay. That the blues tradition can live on in places like Shelby and Clarksdale, so very far away from the commercial interpretations that now pass for blues, is a tribute to the continuing creativity and musical talent of Delta musicians.

The endurance and popularity of this musical form, which developed as a response to the hardship and deprivations of sharecropping around the start of the 20th century, owes much to the blues' universal message of joy and sorrow—a message that cuts across racial, cultural and language barriers. Willie Foster simply says, "What's from the heart reaches the heart."

At a time when the blues is being targeted as a mainstream musical product, one wonders whether the Delta's place in blues history will at least be recognized. In the words of Arthneice Jones:

> *The blues is nothing but a lifestyle,*
> *I'm telling you as simple as it can be.*
> *I didn't choose the blues,*
> *The blues chose me.*

Jim Dickinson, at home, outside Memphis, 1996

Jessie Mae Hemphill, at her trailer park home, outside Clarksdale, 1996

POSTSCRIPT

In April 2011, I revisited Clarksdale as the Mississippi was threatening to burst its banks. The town had moved on since my two earlier visits. John Ruskey, who now runs a canoeing and kayaking business based on the Sunflower River, met me on a paddle board. He directed me to the Ground Zero Blues Club, co-owned by Morgan Freeman, which opened in May 2001. The club provides a safe approximation of juke joints for the ever-increasing number of visitors making Clarksdale their blues destination. I recognized many of the landmarks from a decade ago, but more cafes and shops had opened in the city center grid that clearly caters to a music tourist audience. An Australian flag flew proudly over one of the town's central businesses. It was explained to me that Australian blues fans come in large numbers, and are regular visitors throughout the year, particularly during the Sunflower River Blues and Gospel Festival, which attracted around 20,000 visitors for its 25th anniversary festival in 2012.

BLUES
ARTISTS

B B King, New Orleans Jazz and Heritage Festival, 2010

BOBBY BLUE BLAND

27 January, 1930 – 23 June, 2013

My good friend, colleague and occasional mentor, London photographer David Redfern, always raved about live shows by two artists: Al Green and Bobby Blue Bland. I knew him to be right about Al Green (he was also my all-time favorite live performer), but I didn't get a chance to see Bobby Blue Bland until 2004 in New Orleans. Unfortunately, the sound was hugely problematic that night—it was all over the place and the microphone or PA kept cutting out. This was very unusual in New Orleans; sound quality is normally exceptional. Nonetheless, there was enough in the show to give me an inkling of what the man of song (and with a working PA) can do.

His voice was as smooth as treacle; one of those timeless soul/R&B vocals that forces your feet to start tapping and your hips to start moving. He also turns those dulcet tones to the

blues, coaxing the sweetest and saddest emotions from a vocal style that also mines the pure sounds of gospel. And then there's the snort; he makes this extraordinary mid-vocal sound that can only be described as the kind of thing you would do if you attempted to imitate a pig in mid-song. That's Bobby Blue Bland.

Bobby Blue Bland never achieved the kind of success a man with his prodigious talent deserved, but he did not go unrecognized. He was inducted into the Blues Hall of Fame in 1981, the Rock and Roll Hall of Fame in 1992, and received a Lifetime Achievement Grammy Award in 1997.

ETTA JAMES
25 January, 1938 – 10 January, 2012

Etta James was an extraordinary performer with a history in the music industry that saw her break into the R&B charts in the '50s, have success with ballads and pop in the '60s, embrace soul in the '70s, struggle with her well-documented drug addiction right through until the late '80s, and finally gain recognition as one of the most important artists of her generation in the '90s. What the music history does not tell you is just how down and dirty Etta could be on stage. This woman performed like a soulful sexual predator; she purred like a kitten and used her deep contralto and suggestive body moves to speak straight to the bedroom imaginings of every adult member in the audience.

Etta James was a one-of-a-kind. She has had success in just about every musical genre, she has struggled with drug addiction and come out at the other end, and she has reaped the rewards of many years of effort in the industry. She had a successful touring and recording career into her 60s and 70s, winning a string of Blues Music and Grammy Awards and being inducted into the Blues Hall of Fame in 2001 and the Rock and Roll Hall of Fame in 2003.

In 2009, at the New Orleans Jazz and Heritage Festival, and at the age of 71, she could still hold a large daytime outdoor crowd spellbound, making each and every member of the audience feel like they were in a small smoky nightclub, very late at night, and somewhere between halfway cut or completely stoned. Much slimmer than in previous years (she reportedly lost 200 pounds with the aid of surgery), she was almost unrecognisable. Remaining seated (or perhaps more accurately writhing seated) throughout the performance, she demonstrated that big or small, she was still capable of the most suggestive moves and outrageous behaviour; skilled enough as a performer and sure enough as a world-wise woman to remain just within the furthest boundaries of good taste.

Etta's death from leukaemia in 2012 confirmed she would never reach the heights of popular or mainstream success she may have deserved, but her cult status lives on.

Etta James,
New Orleans Jazz and Heritage Festival,
2009 *(left)*, 1994 *(centre)* and 1998 *(right)*

ROBERT CRAY
Born 1 August, 1953

Robert Cray has firmly established himself at the head of the pack of contemporary bluesmen. Emerging in the 1980s, and building a strong following during that decade in Europe, Cray provides a smooth and seamless transition from the era of Albert Collins, John Lee Hooker and B.B. King through to the next generation of blues men and women.

Cray has picked up four Grammy Awards in his own right including Best Traditional Blues Recording (for *Showdown!*) in 1986; Best Contemporary Blues Recording (for *Strong Persuader*) in 1987; Best Contemporary Blues Recording (for *Don't Be Afraid Of The Dark*) in 1988; and Best Contemporary Blues Album (for *Take Your Shoes Off*) in 1999. In 1996 he shared the Best Rock Instrumental Performance award with Art Neville, B.B. King, Bonnie Raitt, Buddy Guy, Dr. John, Eric Clapton and Jimmie Vaughan (for 'SRV shuffle').

I first met Cray in London back in the mid-80s when his star was rising. I was commissioned for a portrait session for Q magazine and I was immediately impressed with Cray gentlemanliness. It isn't always so easy to wander the streets of London in search of a suitable location for a magazine portrait, but Cray was relaxed, understanding and very good company.

In 1994, I was the only photographer to brave torrential rain to photograph Cray at the New Orleans Jazz and Heritage Festival. As thunder growled and the skies opened up, Cray had just launched into 'The Forecast Calls for Pain'. Wrapped in make-do plastic bags and holding a hopelessly inadequate umbrella in one hand, I am sure I heard Cray changed the lyric that day to 'the forecast calls for rain'.

Years later, in 2009, I photographed Cray again in New Orleans. During this set there was just one 1/125th of a second (or perhaps less, I can't remember if the light that day permitted me to have a faster shutter speed) in which the defining image of the day could be taken. I was on hand, in focus and alert to the moment that day, and I doubt I will ever get a better picture of Robert Cray in full flight.

Robert Cray,
New Orleans Jazz and Heritage Festival, 2009

Facing Page: Robert Cray,
New Orleans Jazz and Heritage Festival,
2004 *(top);* 1994 *(left and centre)* and 2009 *(right)*

WILLIAM JAMES FOSTER
19 September, 1921 – 20 May, 2001

If ever there was a person who personified the blues, then Willie Foster is the man. Known around his Mississippi hometown of Greenville as 'the godfather of the blues', Willie Foster played his blues harmonica with greats such as Muddy Waters, Jimmy Reed, Howlin' Wolf and Little Walter in the 1950s and 60s.

When I met Willie at his Greenville home in 1996, he had resurrected his career with international and national touring—including celebrity status in New Zealand. The following extract is taken from the 1996 'Rebirth of the Blues' piece written and photographed for the *Good Weekend* magazine (*Sydney Morning Herald* and *The Age* newspapers, Australia), which is reproduced in full at the beginning of this section:

At 75, he is the living embodiment of the original blues man. "I was born in the blues and raised in the blues. I've had all kind of blues from the broken-toenail blues to the last-strand-of-hair-in-my-head blues. As low as I am and tall as I am. In other words, I've had the hungry blues, the hurtin' blues, the hard-workin' blues, the couldn't-go-to-school blues."

"The name blues," he explains, "is from 'I'm blue'. We put the 'ues' to it when you feelin' down and out. You feel sad and blue and hurting. That puts a burden on your mind and makes you feel blue. The blues is an inspiration to keep you from crying because you're tired."

That day I spent with Willie at his home was memorable for all sorts of reasons. Rarely have I encountered such warmth and friendship from someone who has suffered so much. Here was a man who had lost his sight and one leg (he was later to lose his other leg), but remained positive and optimistic. He taught me the direct link between the sounds and rhythms of working in the cotton field and the blues music that he made his lifelong work. And he helped me take what I hope are some suitably memorable photographs.

Willie Foster died in a hotel room in Tennessee as a blues man should—after playing a rousing set at a private party earlier that evening.

Left and Right:
Willie Foster, at home in Greenville, 1996

Marcia Ball,
WWOZ Piano Night,
New Orleans, 2004

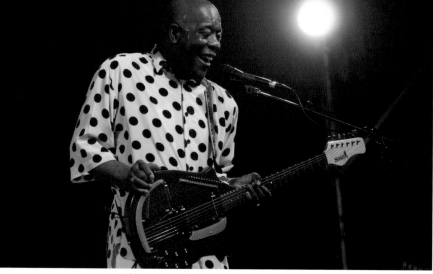

Buddy Guy, House of Blues, New Orleans, 2009

James Cotton, New Orleans Jazz and Heritage Festival, 2012

Ruthie Foster, New Orleans Jazz and Heritage Festival, 2011

Ruth Brown, New Orleans Jazz and Heritage Festival, 1998

Sonny Landreth, New Orleans Jazz and Heritage Festival, 2011

Taj Mahal, New Orleans Jazz and Heritage Festival, 2007

Top Left to Right: Chris Thomas King, New Orleans Jazz and Heritage Festival, 2005; R. L. Burnside, New Orleans Jazz and Heritage Festival, circa 1995; Little Milton, New Orleans Jazz and Heritage Festival, 1995; Charlie Musselwhite, New Orleans Jazz and Heritage Festival, 2011

Bottom Left to Right: John Mayall, New Orleans Jazz and Heritage Festival, 2009; Jimmy Witherspoon, New Orleans, circa 1997; Joss Stone, New Orleans Jazz and Heritage Festival, 2007; Susan Tedeschi, New Orleans Jazz and Heritage Festival, 2005; James "Blood" Ulmer, Ponderosa Stomp, New Orleans, 2002; Keb Mo, New Orleans Jazz and Heritage Festival, 1997; Ben Harper, New Orleans Jazz and Heritage Festival, 2003

WORLD MUSIC

Fela Kuti and Queens, Brixton Academy, London, circa 1990

THE "BIRTH" OF "WORLD" MUSIC

World Music is a label with very little meaning; if anything it could easily be critiqued as a patronizing aggregation of all non-Western musical forms, a simplified catch-all for anything unfamiliar or outside the commercial mainstream. But that would ignore the positive impact of the world music movement in exposing some of the world's best musicians to new and wider audiences.

Prior to 1982, there was very little interest in what we now call world music. The term wasn't adopted as a marketing tool or a genre descriptor until the summer of that year, when the first World of Music, Arts and Dance (WOMAD) festival took place in England and World Music Day (Fête de la Musique) commenced in France.

Peter Gabriel, an English musician with a rock pedigree going back to stadium rock band Genesis, had been experimenting in studio and concert collaborations, particularly with African musicians, from his base in Bristol. In 1980 he co-founded the WOMAD organization, which has since been instrumental in spreading global sounds to audiences all over the world. They were years ahead of the music world in recognizing "that people all over the world would share their enthusiasm for music from other cultures, if only they had the opportunity to listen to some of the global sounds."

WOMAD however, very nearly died at birth. The first WOMAD festival was in 1982 at a horticultural showground in a place called Shepton Mallet, in the English countryside of Somerset, about 10 miles as the crow flies from the more famous site of the Glastonbury Festival. About 2,000–2,500 people attended, attracted primarily by the headline acts of Gabriel himself, Echo and the Bunnymen and ska band the British Beat. None of us, for I was among the festival-goers, knew anything much about the visiting acts that had been lined up. And none of us would have anticipated that this weekend would change the face of the English and world music scene, and music festivals, forever.

This first festival was a commercial disaster. WOMAD would have fallen over if Gabriel had not persuaded Genesis to perform at a fundraiser, but the impact of the Drummers of Burundi, the stand-out international act from that first festival, will reverberate through the years as the time that world music first worked its way into the musical subconscious of an uninitiated English public ready to explore and understand new sounds. Basically, what happened was this. The Drummers of Burundi pounded out such a powerful rhythm that the crowd, having never heard anything like it before, couldn't get the rhythms out of our heads, hips, hands and feet. After Echo and the Bunnymen completed their evening concert, all of the approximately 2,000 people camping onsite were walking around strumming fingers, tapping sticks, banging pans, unable to let go of what we had just heard.

A small group of new friends from Bristol I was camping with started rounding up others in the campsite, and within a matter of minutes our numbers had swelled to hundreds. Everyone was banging sticks, frying pans, tent pegs, saucepans—whatever came to hand. We moved to a small stage adjacent to the camping area; it was probably about 15 feet deep and 45 feet wide, with a back wall about 9 or 12 feet high. Within minutes, the whole campsite was joining in. Two thousand people spontaneously playing rhythm. Organically, a frying pan and spoon would set the rhythm and take the lead, and then tent pegs would take over. Lanterns would be swinging in time. It was exhilarating. This was an English crowd and this was not reserved English behaviour. It was liberating and glorious. After an hour or so the festival security had to close this impromptu jam session down, because people had started climbing the back wall of the stage, using it as a drum. This small stage was meant to display a few cows at an annual agricultural show, not support hundreds of pseudo-hippies banging on makeshift drums.

The next day it rained. Every spare tent or space on the showground was filled with people making their own rhythms, and every subsequent music festival since then invariably features drumming workshops or impromptu rhythm sessions of one sort or another, whether scheduled or not. But it all started in Shepton Mallet, and it was the primal playing of hollowed-out tree trunks by the Drummers of Burundi that lit the spark.

Drummers of Burundi, Shepton Mallet WOMAD, 1982

WORLD
& LATIN
ARTISTS

Tito Puente, Hammersmith Palais, London, circa 1992

FELA ANIKULAPO KUTI

15 October, 1938—2 August, 1997

I am always surprised how few people have heard of Fela Kuti. He was a larger than life character who left an indelible footprint on world music and West African politics. He invented Afrobeat—a hypnotically danceable mix of jazz, funk and high life rhythms—and led, through his music, a popular resistance and emancipation movement against successive Nigerian dictatorships for which he was repeatedly arrested, imprisoned and beaten.

His funeral, in Lagos in 1997, reportedly attracted more than one million mourners. Seun Kuti, a young boy at the time, recounted to me many year later how he could never forget the huge crowds and the outpouring of emotion, and how the funeral procession took the better part of eight hours to traverse a short distance through the capital.

Musically, Fela built a rich and layered sound which still stands the test of time; it is just as danceable now as it was when it was first recorded, and is regularly sampled by contemporary artists looking for new and exciting grooves and rhythms to build on. Some of the world's most influential artists—Stevie Wonder, Bootsy Collins, Gilberto Gil, Paul McCartney, Eryka Badu, King Sunny Ade, Hugh Masakela, the Red Hot Chili Peppers and Brian Eno, to name a few—credit Fela as a major source of inspiration. Two sons, Femi and Seun, are continuing his musical legacy on the world stage; Seun has even picked up his father's Egypt 80 band to record and tour.

Probably what makes the Fela Kuti sound so irresistible is the unique combination of jazz instrumentation (he used multiple baritone saxophones, for example) to build complex but very accessible soundscapes and song cycles that build in waves and patterns over seemingly endlessly deep African grooves. All this is held together by the wickedly irresistible dance beat of band leader and master drummer Tony Allen.

Fela's music is usually repetitive, but never boring; it manages to seamlessly link traditional African poly-rhythms with deep funk, and blends call-and-response vocal and instrumental patterns with 'out there' jazz, reminiscent of highly experimental avant-garde and improvised jazz at its most technically proficient. It is music for the mind and soul, and most definitely for the body; Fela oozed sexual energy and his many dancers (27 of whom he married simultaneously in 1978 and then later divorced in 1986, saying "no man has the right to own a women's vagina") created a spectacle that fairly reeked of long hot and steamy nights in the legendary Shrine nightclub that was Fela's live Lagos base for many years.

Over the top of these musical foundations is the unmistakable voice of Fela; chanting, ranting or advocating in pidgin English everything from high-end political commentary through to low-end pop psychology. The use of pidgin English, from a man who had travelled to England and the USA for education, was a political statement in itself, rejecting the primacy of English over local languages, and thereby reaching out to all Africans throughout the continent.

Fela was just too big and forceful a personality for anyone to reign him in. It may have been his excessive dope smoking (in 1997 he became the only Nigerian 'officially permitted' to smoke marijuana) or his continuous beatings at the hands of Nigerian authorities, but whatever the cause, moderation or consistency could not be expected from this rambling and chaotic counter-cultural genius. Fela's insistence that he maintain his artistic integrity by only recording longer compositions, and only playing live music that he had not previously recorded, limited his opportunities for radio airplay and made it impossible to promote recordings through the time-honored fashion of live touring.

A few years prior to January 1984, the extraordinary evening on which I first saw Fela, he had teamed up with his personal magician and spiritual guide, Professor Hindu (aka Kwaku Addaie, a Ghanaian man). The venue for this 1984 gig was the Belsize Park Country Club. It is a small unassuming venue tucked behind the row of buildings facing Belsize Park tube station, about two thirds of the way up Haverstock Hill and one stop shy of Hampstead Heath in north London. In the fifteen-odd years I covered music gigs all over the city of London, this was the one and only time I had visited this club. There could have been no more than about 120 people in a small room. It was a freezing cold January evening, but hot and steamy inside. Fela sat imperiously at one of the tables, happy to have me bang a flash off in his face for a simple portrait that was the only thing simple or uncomplicated about that particular night.

Professor Hindu took the stage bare-chested—wearing only what appeared to be swimming trunks, an elaborate necklace and shoes and socks. He performed some unimpressive magic with playing cards and made as if to cut his own tongue; this was all very surreal and amateurish, but nonetheless entertaining, even if a little bemusing. A volunteer was then brought to the stage, coaxed into a trance-like state and, to the shock and disbelief of everyone present, Hindu held the man down and appeared to slash his throat with a cleaver. Blood spattered everywhere and pandemonium reigned; the man was carried outside and buried in a shallow grave that had been dug earlier in the grounds of the club. This was January in London, the man was wearing only shorts, and the temperature must have been barely above freezing—the ground itself was effectively frozen and the shallow grave must have taken quite some digging.

As these were the early days of my photographic career, I was using on-camera flash to supplement low light. Sometimes, however, the content of the image is so singularly unique that what matters most is not so much artistic interpretation, but that an accurate record of what is happening is made. This, I think was one of those occasions.

I was not able to return to Belsize Park for the exhumation, but a fellow photographer did, and the *NME* used that picture in a small article buried at the back of the following week's edition—the only contemporary record of this bizarre event. An *Observer* article that appeared in August 2004 took up the story: "Two days later 200 people witnessed the volunteer's disinterment; he [Professor Hindu] explained that being buried makes people extremely horny and propositioned the music journalist Vivien Goldman, pleading: 'I have money. Plenty money' and waving a hotel key."

In 2014, the 'Finding Fela' documentary included video footage of this event for the first time. I did not remember the event being filmed, and if I am honest, I was disappointed that this video footage existed—it robbed me of any claim that my images are the unique surviving record. Of course, as time passes the idea that anybody is likely to have exclusive or unique images or recordings of any event is increasingly unlikely; what probably matters now is how and when these images are used, and whether the images are strong enough on their own to endure the passage of time.

The next time I saw Fela, some six years later, was altogether different. It was a very big show—possibly 1500 to 2,000 people—at the Brixton Academy in south London. In the intervening time, Fela had become seriously hip. Local pirate radio station Kiss FM, now licensed and commercial, promoted the concert. The Kiss-targeted 18–35-year-old London demographic had seemingly developed an insatiable appetite for dance rhythms and grooves.

The stage was large and the show impressive. Fela orchestrated both the big band and the full complement of his wives and dancers; I don't think anything quite like this had been seen in London previously. Fela also ranted in what I vaguely remember as an odd and disconnected polemic linking cigarette smoking, global capitalism and political dictatorship. As a political platform it was bizarre and unconvincing, as a concert and performance it was nothing less than mesmerising; arguably one of the most important and influential live performances in London in that formative period for world and dance music.

The dance music scene that now anointed Fela as its spiritual guru and rhythm master also spawned or supported a range of influential British jazz-influenced soul and dance artists including Soul II Soul, Galliano, Brand New Heavies, Courtney Pine and Jamiroquai. As for Fela's political significance, it is almost impossible for someone who does not know or understand the Nigerian political scene to comment with any authority. This much appears uncontested. At the height of his popularity in the mid-70s, when Fela set up his alternative commune in the Kalakuta ('Rascal') Republic compound, and performed each night in the Shrine, his perennially popular Lagos nightclub, Fela was repeatedly harassed, beaten and arrested by the Nigerian authorities. Around this time he took to calling himself the 'Black President', and in 1979 formed the Movement of the People Party, but was thwarted from standing for election as President by the powers that be. It is probably a leap too far to think that this counter-cultural revolutionary might have become a leader of his nation, but Fela's popularity was both widespread and genuine. If political power and influence can be measured by the level of attention from the military authorities, then Fela was a heavyweight.

Fela's popularity was built on a potent mix of the originality of his music, the subversiveness of his openly defiant lifestyle and the associated message for the poor African masses. Fela's

protest message was uncompromising; few other protest singers of any ilk have so directly challenged the authorities. His hit album from 1977, *Zombie*, mocked the military and spread like wildfire across Africa. Nigerian authorities reacted with unprecedented violence. A thousand soldiers attacked his Kalakuta compound, burning and destroying the buildings, the recording studio and all of Fela's master tapes. (This was the same compound that was nearly destroyed in 1974 during an earlier arrest.) Fela suffered a fractured skull, arm and leg, and is said to have narrowly escaped death thanks only to the intervention of an army general. Fela's 82-year-old mother was not so fortunate; she was thrown from an upstairs window and subsequently died from the injuries sustained. Many of the women were brutally raped and Fela chose voluntary exile in Ghana for his recovery. The Ghanaian authorities eventually grew weary of hosting this popular political activist, and Fela was deported back to Lagos the following year.

From 1980 to 1983, Fela recorded and toured extensively while Nigeria was under civilian rule. When the military returned to power in 1983, Fela was again imprisoned, this time for five years, on the basis of a trumped-up charge of currency smuggling when returning from an overseas tour. He was released in 1986 following an international human rights campaign led by Amnesty International and many of his global supporters and admirers.

Fela's prolific recording and touring slowed in his later years, and the significance of Fela's legacy is now slowly being unravelled. Posthumous books, exhibitions and performance tributes have been written, curated and performed. Two of his sons have picked up their father's musical and political Afrobeat batons; a New York musical opened on Broadway in November 2009; and a documentary, weaving together the story of the development of the stage musical with the story of his life, was released in 2014.

In life, Fela always flirted with death and spirituality, but considered himself invincible. He changed his name to Anikulapo ('one who carries death in the pouch'), saying "I can't die; they can't kill me." They couldn't, but disease—or perhaps one beating too many—could. Fela Anikulapo Kuti died in Lagos at the age of 59, from complications arising from AIDS. As his Nigerians followers will tell you, they now have two pictures on their wall, Jesus Christ and Fela Anikulapo Kuti: "Jesus died for our sins and Fela died for Africa."

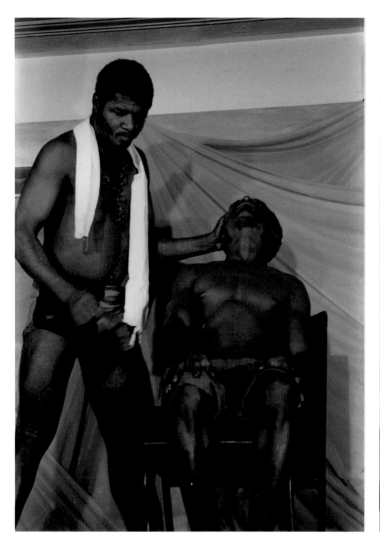
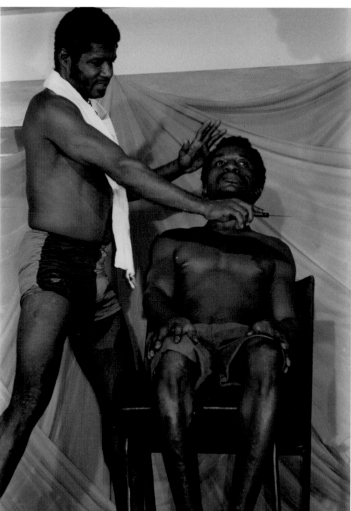

Belsize Park Country Club, London, 1984: In this unassuming venue, Fela Kuti introduced his personal magician and spiritual guide, Professor Hindu (aka Kwaku Addaie). Professor Hindu performed some unimpressive magic with playing cards and then coaxed a volunteer into a trance-like state. The pictures tell what happened next: Hindu held the man down and appeared to slash the man's throat with a cleaver. He was then carried outside and buried in a shallow grave. Two days later, 200 people witnessed the volunteer's disinterment.

MIRIAM MAKEBA
4 March, 1932 – 10 November, 2008

Miriam Makeba, or 'Mama Africa' as she became known, was the pre-eminent South African artist in exile during the apartheid years. Her singing talent took her to the world's stage almost unwittingly; she considered her singing as giving voice to the lives of ordinary South Africans rather than being a political statement. Similarly, she professed no premeditated musical genius in successfully combining township jive with jazz for the first time. In her mind, she was just singing songs.

Makeba first entered the United States with the support, guidance and assistance of the man she always described as her brother, Harry Belafonte. He had taken her under his wing after they met in London in 1959, following an earlier appearance at the Venice Film Festival to assist in the promotion of an anti-apartheid documentary. Together they received, in 1996, the Grammy Award for Best Folk Recording, making Makeba the first African woman to win a Grammy. Their winning album, *An Evening With Belafonte/Makeba*, specifically addressed apartheid issues in South Africa.

The two songs she contributed to Lionel Rogosin's 1959 anti-apartheid documentary *Come Back, Africa* precipitated a tumultuous and often tragic long-term exile from her home country. In 1960 she attempted to return to South Africa for her mother's funeral, only to find her passport had been revoked. Three years later, after she testified against the apartheid regime before the United Nations, her citizenship was revoked.

I had the great privilege of seeing Makeba perform at a night concert at the 1994 New Orleans Jazz and Heritage Festival with one of her four ex-husbands, South African trumpeter and fellow leading light in the anti-apartheid movement, Hugh Masakela. In the review of that festival I wrote for the *Good Weekend* magazine (which is published with the *Sydney Morning Herald* and *Melbourne Age*), I wrote "Miriam Makeba and Hugh Masakela perform with a poignancy of spirit that reflects Miriam's simple statement: 'I've just celebrated my sixty-second birthday and I've been in exile for thirty-five years. Next week I go home to vote.'" This was an extraordinarily momentous occasion. So intrinsically intertwined with the anti-apartheid struggle was Makeba's life that it is difficult to separate the emotions of the anti-apartheid political victory from the significance of Makeba's musical legacy.

With the benefit of hindsight, I think it is fair to claim that Makeba changed the way the world understood music. Her two big hits of the '60s, 'Pata Pata' and the 'Click Song', are essentially township dance songs; they are infectiously danceable tunes, perhaps more palatable to Western ears than some of the more raw township jive that was being produced at that time. What Makeba did with these songs was to introduce a new sensitivity to Western ears; a sensitivity that emphasized the importance of dance and the sheer physicality of joyous and uplifting music. In doing this she paved the way for what we now celebrate as world music. It is probably not surprising then, that her *Homeland* album, released in 2000 after her return to South Africa from exile, was nominated for a Grammy Award in the Best World Music category.

Makeba's life was peppered with tragedy and high drama that perhaps only another high-profile exile might understand. After her early successes in the USA, she fell in love with and married the radical activist, Stokely Carmichael, in 1968. 1968 was a volatile year for worldwide student and worker protests, anti-Vietnam protests and heightened civil rights activism in the USA. This marriage incurred the wrath of the music industry. Touring and recording opportunities were quickly closed down and the couple moved to Guinea, a country where her greatest personal tragedy occurred in 1985, when Makeba's only daughter died from complications associated with a miscarriage.

Music remained the driving force in Makeba's life and she used her status to campaign for AIDS awareness and against injustice, not just in Africa, but wherever she saw it. She was campaigning for the right to speak out against the Mafia when she died during a concert in Caserta, Italy. In response to an obituary published in the *Economist* magazine, a poignant comment (by one Jose Carpintero) was posted on the magazine's web site on 13 November 2008:

> Miriam died on stage, as she finished her last song (she had skip five songs of the playlist agreed with the band, as if she knew there wasn't much time left). What a fitting way to finish an exemplary life. My standing ovation.

Miriam Makeba, New Orleans Jazz and Heritage Festival, 1994

CELIA CRUZ
21 October, 1925 – 16 July, 2003

Celia Cruz, the 'Queen of Salsa' and 'La Guarachera de Cuba', was a wonderfully vibrant performer who personified the joy and rhythm of salsa, rhumba and Latin American music. Hugely popular among exiled Cubans living in the USA—she left post-revolution Cuba permanently in 1960—she also had a huge fan base in the Latin and Caribbean world. In 1995, Billboard magazine awarded her its lifetime achievement award, describing her as "undisputedly the best-known and most influential female figure in the history of Afro-Cuban music."

Her career took off in 1950 when she joined the famous Cuban band, La Sonora Matanzera, travelling throughout Latin America and becoming known as 'Café Con Leche' (coffee with milk). Her famous catch cry, "¡Azúcar!" (Spanish for sugar!), had its origins in a story she would tell about ordering coffee in Miami, and a waiter asking her if she wanted sugar in her coffee. She replied that he should know you can't drink Cuban coffee without sugar! As her career and international reputation progressed, there was no longer any need for the story; the catch cry had a life if its own and fans would delight in shouting "A—zu—car!" to a resplendent Ms Cruz.

Over the years Cruz collaborated with a range of major Latin and more mainstream artists including Johnny Pacheco, Tito Puente, Ray Baretto, Caetano Veloso, Patti LaBelle, Wyclef Jean, Emilio Estefan, Luciano Pavarotti, and David Byrne (on the soundtrack to the 1986 film *Something Wild*). In 1992, she was cast as a nightclub owner in the film *The Mambo Kings*, alongside Andy Garcia and Antonio Banderas. Throughout her career she achieved twenty-three gold records, was awarded a star on the Hollywood Walk of Fame in 1987, won a Grammy Award with Ray Baretto in 1990 for Best Tropical Latin Performance, and received three consecutive Latin Grammy Awards from the inception of those awards in 2000.

I saw her perform in a Jazz Fest night concert in 1995, and again in a daytime interview and performance at the 2001 festival. She was marvellously alive and vibrant, comfortable with her status as elder stateswoman of Latin music, and both warm and generous in sharing her music and life stories with fans. Music was her life, she told us, and she intended to continue touring indefinitely.

She always sparkled and shone; it was as if she had an internal light that burned with incandescent energy. She looked, sung and moved with a style and panache of a queen—the salsa queen—even into her late 70s. She had one of the widest and most infectious smiles of just about any artist I have seen, and she is certainly the only artist I have known who could carry off large spangled spectacles, a la Dame Edna Everage, without ever appearing gauche or kitsch.

True to her word, Cruz continued to tour with gusto and style right up until her death from a cancerous brain tumour at her home in Fort Lee, New Jersey in July of 2003. She had requested that her funeral include two public viewings: one in New York, the city she adopted as home, and one in Miami, the city which adopted her, on behalf of the two million plus Cuban exiles living in the USA.

In February 2004, her album *Regalo del Alma*, released after her death, won a posthumous award at the Premios Lo Nuestro (Univision Television's Latin Music Awards) as best Salsa release of the year. On May 18, 2005, the National Museum of American History in Washington, D.C. opened "*¡Azúcar!*", an exhibition celebrating the life and music of Celia Cruz. The exhibition includes 'Celia Cruz's Shoes 1997', with the following caption:

The "Queen of Salsa"

These custom-made, gold vinyl platform shoes designed by Mexican shoemaker Mr. Nieto, were worn by the legendary Cuban singer Celia Cruz, who died on July 16, 2003. Known internationally as the "Queen of Salsa," and "*La Guarachera de Cuba*," these shoes were one of her trademarks. Born the second of four children in the barrio Santo Suarez of Havana, Cuba, Celia Cruz moved to the U.S. in 1960 and became one of the most important singers of the 20th century. In 1997, Celia Cruz donated one of her stage costumes, a *bata cubana*—which includes these shoes—to the Smithsonian. In 2001 she was awarded one of the Smithsonian's highest honors, the Smithson Medal, in recognition of her contributions to the increase and diffusion of knowledge.

¡Azúcar!

Far Left: Celia Cruz, La Noche Latina, New Orleans Jazz and Heritage Festival, 1995
Near Left, Top and Bottom: Celia Cruz, New Orleans Jazz and Heritage Festival, 2001

Salif Keita, WOMADelaide, Adelaide, 2013

Hugh Masakela, New Orleans Jazz and Heritage Festival, 2009

Youssou N'Dour, Town and Country Club, London, circa 1991

Seun Kuti, New Orleans Jazz and Heritage Festival, 2012

King Sunny Ade, New Orleans Jazz and Heritage Festival, 2000

Ali Farka Toure, London, circa 1992

Ruben Blades, New Orleans Jazz and Heritage Festival, 2014

Arturo Sandoval, New Orleans Jazz and Heritage Festival, 2007

Soweto Street Beat, New Orleans Jazz and Heritage Festival, 2004

Carlos Santana, New Orleans Jazz and Heritage Festival, 2014

Left, Top to Bottom:
Airto and Flora Purim, New Orleans, circa 2000
Manu Dibango, Town and Country Club, London, circa 1992
Hermeto Pascoal, New Orleans Jazz and Heritage Festival, 2000

Angelique Kidjo, New Orleans Jazz and Heritage Festival, 2015

Right, Top to Bottom:
Ladysmith Black Mambazo, New Orleans Jazz and Heritage Festival, 2002
Poncho Sanchez, New Orleans Jazz and Heritage Festival, 2004
Busi Mhlongo, New Orleans Jazz and Heritage Festival, 2004

GOSPEL

Mississippi Gospel Choir, New Orleans Jazz and Heritage Festival, 2009

Gospel Choir (unidentified) in the gospel tent, New Orleans Jazz and Heritage Festival, circa 2000

Gospel music is the training ground for our greatest vocalists and the bedrock on which much of blues and soul has been built. Of course, gospel is much, much more than this. It is a vibrant and sustaining force for many people's lives, particularly those facing economic or social hardship and for whom the church is central to surviving life's struggles. My experience, even as an outside observer, is that gospel is a thrilling affirmation of faith. It taps into the primal and innate desire and need for humans to connect, share experiences, and support their family or folk in good times and in bad.

The gospel tent at Jazz Fest is where I have had some of my most extraordinary experiences. Artists of the calibre of Raymond Myles, Mighty Clouds of Joy, Mavis Staples and the Blind Boys of Alabama have all performed on this stage. Aaron Neville's guest vocals with the Zion Harmonisers were always the festival's worst-kept secret, and he now performs an advertised

solo set each year; it's as if he is thanking God for bestowing on him this extraordinary gift of a voice. Irma Thomas too, performs most years, reaching back into her gospel roots to pay tribute to Mahalia Jackson, who sang at the very first festival in Congo Square. And Davell Crawford and Glen David Andrews never fail to give inspirational performances when they are performing gospel.

In 2009, the Mississippi Gospel Choir were in full flight. It was the first and only time I have seen this choir. They sounded glorious and looked amazing. And then they did something I have never seen before or since: they swung low. Their bodies bent and swung in devotion—they were 'getting down' for the Lord. The resulting photo has become my favorite gospel image.

In all my years of photographing musicians, I have cried on only three occasions. The last time was in 2009, when the plaintiff call of Wynton Marsalis' trumpet evoked heartbreaking memories of the impacts of Katrina. The first time was over twenty-five years earlier, at a Glastonbury festival in England in the early '80s, when Irish songwriter Christy Moore moved me to tears over the injustice of British oppression towards Irish nationalists. While it was very hard to hold back tears in 1998 when Johnny Adams was singing what was effectively his own requiem with Aaron Neville in the gospel tent, it wasn't until 2004, over twenty years after Christie Moore's performance, that I cried for a second time. 2004 was the year that the festival profiled and programmed South African music and culture as a tribute to the post-apartheid era and to the influence of South African musicians on Louisiana music and culture.

Rebecca Malope is tiny, but she packs more emotional intensity into that little frame than just about any other artist I have ever seen. I hadn't heard of Rebecca Malope prior to the 2004 Jazz Fest, but I am a big fan of South African musicians like Vusi Mahlasela, Hugh Masakela and Mahlatini and the Mahotella Queens, so I was keen to see my first South African gospel performance. I found myself pretty much alone in the shallow photo pit at the front of the gospel stage, and I was enthralled by the energy, vibrancy and commitment of the performance. It was a very peculiar experience—I wasn't just crying, I was weeping. I wasn't sobbing so much as sending tears pouring down my cheeks. I actually did not know I was crying until I started to find it difficult to take pictures (because I couldn't see through the viewfinder). It's hard to explain this—it has not happened before or since—other than to state the obvious: Rebecca Malopehad touched something very deep within.

Gospel musicians, I think, are not just aspiring to rise to musical heights; they are aiming at reaffirming belief, uplifting the soul and invoking the power and wisdom of their Lord. So when it goes off, and it often does, the hairs on the back of your neck stand up. It's a feeling and a sensation that you don't ever forget. The best way I can describe it is to say that during these extraordinary vocal performances of indescribable emotional intensity, even purity, I usually get lost in the moment and tell myself—either at the time or shortly after the event—something along the lines of, "I don't care what it is that is making this happen, but I want to be a part of it."

At Jazz Fest, I will drop in and out of the gospel tent to check who is playing; it's always a good spot to sit and enjoy some musical preaching from the stage pulpit. I always keep an eye out for a choir that wears the old-fashioned gowns. These days most choirs wear printed T-shirts, and it tends not to result in as impressive an image. I try to pick a choir I have particularly enjoyed listening to, and then ask the pastor for permission to attend the next Sunday morning church service. I have never been refused and never been disappointed. The church is normally evangelical in its embrace of visitors. An international visitor is a special guest, and when that international guest is also a photographer, the choir normally sees this as a vindication of their praise for their Lord.

The only downside of going to church on a Sunday morning is that it is Sunday morning. Saturday night is usually a big night for live music in New Orleans, so it is not unusual to get very little sleep and it's hard not to feel a little tarnished (if that is the right word) when I have been out for much of the night, partying with minimal or no restraint. That said, the church service is always uplifting and the genuine joy of the church congregation welcoming visitors is always heartwarming. I can't help but think they are used to having bleary-eyed visitors and congregants; such is the ongoing and historical tension between gospel and the secular dance and club music it has helped to spawn.

I will offer one little piece of advice to church visitors that dates back to my first visit to a gospel church in New York in 1990. This was around the time that David Dinkins was elected as the first, and so far only, African-American Mayor of that great city. I had been working with Harlem church leaders on one of the back stories to Dinkins' election, and visited one of the larger gospel churches in Harlem as part of that story.

I didn't feel comfortable taking photographs—it just didn't feel right on that particular day—but I enjoyed the service, which was an eye-opener to me. The band were all great musicians, the vocalists were extraordinary, and the sermons were a sonorous reflection of the music in their cadence, rhythm and call to worship. The first time the collection box came around, I was very happy to put a five-dollar bill on the plate that was passed around. The second time, same thing. By the third, fourth and fifth times, I was running out of anything but much larger notes. As a conspicuous outsider, I felt obliged to put something on the tray each time it was passed around. It became a very costly visit. My advice: carry a wallet full of smaller denomination bills.

Aaron Neville and the Zion Harmonisers, New Orleans Jazz and Heritage Festival, circa 2002

My final comment about gospel music is to observe that I think the link between music and spirituality is one of the most profound of human artistic endeavors. In the spectrum of artistic and spiritual ambition, gospel is probably the most direct and uninhibited of musical genres; while jazz, particularly improvised jazz, is probably the most intellectual and aspirational. It is no surprise then, that the two musical forms would come together at New Orleans—they complement each other, they feed into and off each other, and they close the loop on the history of African-American music, creating the greatest new classical music form of the twentieth century: jazz.

Rebecca Malope, New Orleans Jazz and Heritage Festival, 2004

Second Mount Carmel Voices, Second Mount Carmel Baptist Church, New Orleans, 2008

SINGER-
SONG-
WRITER
ARTISTS

Lucinda Williams, New Orleans Jazz and Heritage Festival, 2007

LUCINDA WILLIAMS
Born 26 January, 1953

No-one wears their art on their sleeve quite like Lucinda Williams. There is a depth of raw emotion and uncompromising honesty in her singing and songwriting that inspires devotion from fans and unfettered admiration from musicians and critics alike. Over the years she has moved from simplicity and pared-down production to more lush arrangements and collaborations, but always on what are very much her own terms. Probably no other artist since Bob Dylan, a major inspiration to Williams in her early career, has made such a virtue of combining imperfect vocals and simplicity in songwriting. She is a modern-day folk chronicler of the American south, but her medium is, as she says herself, "too country for rock and too rock for country."

Historically adept at what her website calls "painting landscapes of the soul, illuminating the spirit's shadowy nooks and shimmering crannies," she has previously been labelled "darkly introspective," but on later recordings demonstrates that optimism and hope are now part of her emotional lexicon. Back in 2000, in an interview with *Addicted to Noise*, she said, "I think everybody should be proud of where they're from ... I like to pay homage, it's like a respect thing almost, like being proud of where you're from and proud of your roots."

At the 2007 New Orleans Jazz and Heritage Festival, this Louisiana-born singer–songwriter made her first appearance since Hurricane Katrina in the city in which she went to school and first began her musical career. Everyone knew this would be a very special performance; the large crowd waited expectantly. She poured her heart out, and I wrote at the time that this performance

> might well be the best concert she will ever perform. She tells the adoring audience that she has locked herself in her touring bus for two days to prepare herself for this gig. "I went to high school in New Orleans in the 60s—this is one of the greatest cities in the world and I'm honored to perform here". At the conclusion of 'Everything has changed', her voice cracks: "That one really broke me up."

Lucinda Williams is not the easiest artist to photograph; she is not overly active or demonstrative on stage, and the challenge is to capture an image that goes beyond Lucinda standing at the microphone and playing guitar. The pictures from that very memorable concert in 2007, evidence, I think, of a spiritual reverence that is not always so obvious in Lucinda's persona.

Lucinda Williams has won three Grammy Awards, including Best Country Song in 1993 for the Mary Chapin recording of 'Passionate Kisses'— the standout song on her third and self-titled album; Best Contemporary Folk Album in 1998 for *Car Wheels On A Gravel Road*; and Best Female Rock Vocal Performance in 2001 for 'Get Right with God'. In 2002, *Time* magazine named Lucinda Williams "America's best songwriter."

Left: Lucinda Williams, New Orleans Jazz and Heritage Festival, 2001
Right: Lucinda Williams, New Orleans Jazz and Heritage Festival, 2003

MICHAEL FRANTI
Born 21 April, 1966

Michael Franti might just be the last in a long line of American troubadours and musical poets of political conscience. In an era when the music and creative industries are characterized more by their commercial intent than the embrace of some form of greater good, and in which Bob Dylan prefers to disavow any political intent in his protest postures from the 60s, it has been left to Michael Franti to keep alive the tradition of contemporary popular musician as social advocate.

Franti's avowed mission in life "to make a difference" first began to materialise through the politically charged rap of the Disposable Heroes of Hiphoprisy, but has now grown into something that resembles a global youth movement for social change. This is all fuelled by Franti's 'conscious lyrics' and an irresistible blend of foot-stomping reggae, funk, hip hop and calypso-tinged folk. It is danceable, clubbable and listenable. And it speaks to those of a new generation who want to believe that music can and will, banish indifference.

Franti is a talented songwriter and musician. His lyrics are both poignant and uplifting. He speaks directly to "all the freaky people" who Franti says "make the beauty of the world." He offers an attractive alternative to the pressure, competitiveness and isolation of mainstream society, and has a rare capacity and skill to directly connect with youthful angst, frustrations and aspirations. 'Yes I Will', a song from his 2003 album Everyone Deserves Music, is a good example:

> I believe that what you sing to the clouds,
>
> Will rain upon you when your sun has gone away,
>
> And I believe that what you dream to the moon,
>
> Will manifest before you rest another day. ...
>
> When you're lost and alone that's when a rainbow comes for you.

While the hippy overtones of peace and love and group hugs can at times make you think that this must be some lingering influence from the San Francisco experiment of the '60s (Franti was born across the bay in Oakland in 1966), it is difficult to do anything other than admire Franti's honesty and commitment.

I have seen Franti perform on numerous occasions, and I am always struck by the power of the performance and the devotional response he engenders. A few years prior to Katrina he was billed to come on one night at Tipitina's at one a.m. I turned up to find 'all the freaky people' lined up around the block—it was going to be a big night and tickets to this gig had sold out weeks before. The crowd wasn't let into the venue until about two am, and Franti didn't turn up until about four am. None of this seemed to concern any of his fans—everyone was just overjoyed to worship at the altar of Michael Franti and Spearhead.

In 2009, Franti was billed to perform at the People's Festival at the Martin Luther King, Jr. Charter School in the Lower Ninth Ward on the Saturday evening of the second weekend of Jazz Fest. Franti had offered at the previous festival to do a free performance for people still struggling with the aftermath of Katrina, and here he was, barefooted as always, delivering on that offer. (He puts his money and his time where his outspoken mouth is; he makes a habit of delivering on offers of support for worthy causes of one sort or another.)

This festival was a local affair, organised by a collection of grassroots non-profit groups to celebrate the resilience and determination of those people who had come home to rebuild a part of New Orleans totally devastated by Hurricane Katrina. A series of local performers and a samba band and Brazilian dance group preceded the more famous headliner. The school stage, not coincidentally, had a full-size backdrop featuring a striking portrait of Martin Luther King, Jr. It was a memorable night, and I like to think a fitting image of a unique American who continues to fight for social justice in the only way he knows how: through music.

Michael Franti,
People's Festival, Martin Luther King, Jr. Charter School,
Lower Ninth Ward, New Orleans, 2009

Emmylou Harris, New Orleans Jazz and Heritage Festival, 2009

India.Arie, New Orleans Jazz and Heritage Festival, 2004

Odetta, New Orleans Jazz and Heritage Festival, 2002

Top Left: Chaka Khan, New Orleans Jazz and Heritage Festival, 2014
Top Right: Randy Newman, New Orleans Jazz and Heritage Festival, 1994

Bottom, From Left to Right: Sade, ICA, London, 1982; Elvis Costello, New Orleans Jazz and Heritage Festival, 2010; Lyle Lovett, New Orleans Jazz and Heritage Festival, 2014; John Legend, New Orleans Jazz and Heritage Festival, 2011; Ani DiFranco, New Orleans Jazz and Heritage Festival, 2012; Pete Seeger, New Orleans Jazz and Heritage Festival, 1995; Willie Nelson, New Orleans Jazz and Heritage Festival, 1994

REGGAE

Steel Pulse, New Orleans Jazz and Heritage Festival, 2012

Steel Pulse, Birmingham, circa 1992

The first time I came across reggae was at a party in Perth, Australia, when I was about eighteen. It would have been my first or second year as a University student, probably about 1975 or 1976. Bob Marley was playing on the turntable and this was a sound I hadn't heard before. There was something about the rhythm that caught you in a groove and wouldn't let go. As we wandered through the house, a lone naked man was dancing to the music in the backyard. Somehow you don't forget an image like that.

A few years later I was producing and editing a student newspaper at what is now Curtin University in Perth. This was when I was just beginning to learn the art of photography, and our newspaper had a big emphasis on music. Bob Marley was coming to town, and we headed off into the city for a press conference.

The press conference was stultifying. The local media had no idea who or what reggae was, and a very regal Bob Marley endured a few inane questions and then walked out. He was intercepted on his way out by a young Jamaican who had recently returned from home; he had smuggled into Australia some of the very best Jamaican grass, and took Marley aside to explain to him in patois what it was he had to offer the great man. Marley's face lit up and beamed a huge smile—he disappeared with the young Jamaican in tow.

Bob Marley was on fire that night and the concert was performed under a cloud of exhaled marijuana smoke from thousands of young Australians in the concert venue. A non-smoker could not escape—the air was thick and pungent with the smell of ganga. In retrospect, I regret not taking photographs at that concert, or even at the press conference, but I was only just beginning to learn the craft and it was safer to leave it to one of my more experienced colleagues.

Some years later, when I landed in London in the early 1980s, reggae was one of the soundtracks for the city. English reggae acts like Aswad, Misty in Roots and Brown Sugar were performing in concerts and outdoor events, and ska and reggae was filtering through to the

Stephen Marley,
New Orleans Jazz and
Heritage Festival, 2007

pop charts through bands like UB40. I became close friends with the Dread Broadcasting Corporation, London's first pirate radio station, which personified reggae and introduced me to the Notting Hill Carnival sound systems that would play calypso, soca and reggae.

During this period I photographed many English acts and visiting Jamaican artists like Horace Andy, Michael Palmer, Michigan and Smiley, Barry Biggs and Gregory Isaacs. Reggae concerts and artists were very hard work. Jamaican time is very elastic and I can't recall one concert starting within an hour of the advertised time or one artist turning up to a photo session on time. But once that bass and drums kicked in, the one drop of the rhythm took over and it was impossible not to move to the beat.

I visited Birmingham to photograph UB40 for a magazine cover, but only two of the band members turned up. I photographed Maxi Priest in South London before he became well known, and somewhere in my archive is a photograph of Maxi in shorts (he is probably thankful I have left it where it is). Around this time, dub poetry was becoming very hip. Michael Smith visited London from Jamaica, inspiring British poets like Linton Kwesi Johnson and Benjamin Zephaniah. Michael Smith was tragically murdered in August 1983, a victim of the brutal politics of Jamaica of the time. Poets like Mutabaruka carried on the tradition.

I was also commissioned to photograph one of reggae's most enduring acts, Steel Pulse, in Birmingham, probably around 1990 or 1991. My recollection is that this was either for an album or liner notes, or for publicity images to go with the launch of an album. I set up a makeshift studio in one of the band member's front rooms and took large-format portraits which I remember as being strong and well lit—but have never seen the images since; I must have handed over the original transparencies. I also did some location photography around Birmingham. I recollect a car museum or exhibition of some sort (musicians seem to like being photographed in flash cars), but my favorite image is one I still have and which I don't think has been previously published.

In an unexceptional street in inner Birmingham, I had the band line up outside what my memory told me was a greengrocer's shop, but on revisiting the photograph over twenty years later, turns out to be a bus stop (the greengrocer's is probably the soft-focus shop in the background). The afternoon wintry light was fading fast, so I adopted a technique that mixes flash with available light. It's a useful technique that can sharpen the main subject and create atmosphere by bringing a little movement into the image. Basically you take a longish exposure, somewhere between a quarter and a full second, and you set the aperture so the background is correctly exposed (or just slightly underexposed). You then bang off a flash, either at the beginning or end of the exposure, just enough to add some fill to light the main subject or subjects. You can move the camera to create some blur, or hold the camera steady so anything moving in the frame creates either a blur or a ghost image of itself.

These days you can check the digital camera back to see how your light and movement is balanced; in those days it was a question of experience, intuition and luck. This photo reminds me of cold and grey Birmingham. I particularly like the quality of the lighting and the movement of the young girls on the footpath. I can't be sure why it wasn't used at the time, but I'm very happy I can bring it to life many years later.

Reggae music is always featured at Jazz Fest, and Steel Pulse has become a regular on the Congo Stage. Over the years artists like Toots, Rita, Julian and Stephen Marley, Burning Spear, Third World and Jimmy Cliff have also performed. This programming is, in my view, a fitting reminder of the Jamaican influence in the melting pot of New Orleans music.

From Top to Bottom:
Luciano, New Orleans Jazz and Heritage Festival, 2005
Rita Marley, New Orleans Jazz and Heritage Festival, 1997
Frederick "Toots" Hibbert, New Orleans Jazz and Heritage Festival, 2005

Facing Page Top
Left: Third World, New Orleans Jazz and Heritage Festival, 2009
Top Right: Gregory Isaacs, London, circa 1990
Middle Right: Burning Spear, New Orleans Jazz and Heritage Festival, 1998

Facing Page Bottom, From Left to Right:
The Abyssinians, New Orleans Jazz and Heritage Festival, 2001
Desmond Dekker, London, 1994
Julian Marley, New Orleans Jazz and Heritage Festival, 2009
Benjamin Zephaniah and Michael Smith, Poetry Olympics, London, circa 1985

JIMMY CLIFF
Born 1 April, 1948

Jimmy Cliff is one of the best known elder statesmen of reggae. He helped reggae gain international exposure when he starred in the 1972 film, *The Harder They Come*, the soundtrack of which includes two of his signature songs, 'The Harder They Come' and 'Many Rivers to Cross', featuring surely the most memorable reggae vocals of all time. I have seen Jimmy Cliff in concert many times and over many years—in London, in New Orleans and in Adelaide—and you can always be assured of a great band, powerful vocals and a stirring performance.

Jimmy Cliff has courted controversy as an outspoken advocate for human rights and is the only living musician to be awarded Jamaica's highest honor, the Order of Merit. In 1985, he was one of several high-profile musicians who formed Artists United Against Apartheid to promote the cultural boycott of South Africa by vowing never to perform at Sun City. Five years earlier, however, Cliff had performed two concerts in South Africa; that decision still rankles with some.

At a Crystal Palace outdoor concert in London—it would have been about 1984—the line-up included Aswad, Jimmy Cliff and Gil Scott-Heron. Gil Scott-Heron did not play that day. The crowd was told that he had missed his flight and could not turn up, but it wasn't true—he was sitting backstage in the demountable set aside for him. I know this to be so because I photographed him there, sitting under his handwritten name, and that image was later used in at least one obituary when he died in 2011. The rumour backstage was that Scott-Heron refused to perform on the same stage as Jimmy Cliff because he had performed in South Africa. It's a plausible explanation, but I can't verify the story one way or the other. There may have been another equally plausible explanation (you never know with the music business) and I never had the chance to ask Gil Scott-Heron for his version.

Either way, Jimmy Cliff could have done little more to redeem himself. In January of 1984, the U.N. Centre Against Apartheid released a statement on the cultural boycott acknowledging that they were keeping

> a list of people who have performed in South Africa because of ignorance of the situation or the lure of money or unconcern over racism. They need to be persuaded to stop entertaining apartheid, to stop profiting from apartheid money and to stop serving the propaganda purposes of the apartheid regime. We also have lists of artists whom we are approaching for co-operation in educating public opinion about apartheid and in organizing performances for the benefit of the oppressed people of South Africa.

If Cliff had been wrong-headed in performing two concerts in 1980, little more could have been asked of him by 1985, when he joined Steven Van Zandt and a stellar list of artists (including Miles Davis, Peter Gabriel, Bonnie Raitt, Bob Dylan, Keith Richards, Bruce Springsteen, Jackson Browne, Afrika Bambaataa, George Clinton, Lou Reed, the Temptations and Run-DMC) to make and release the *Sun City* album and single denouncing apartheid and vowing never to perform in the Sun City resort.

Jimmy Cliff continues to tour, perform and release new reggae albums. He has sustained his commitment to socially conscious lyrics and his extraordinary tenor voice continues to enthral and enchant old and new audiences alike. In 2010 he was inducted into the Rock and Roll Hall of Fame with the following words: "Jimmy Cliff was reggae's first international star and remains its greatest living ambassador."

Jimmy Cliff, Crystal Palace, London, circa 1984
Facing Page: Jimmy Cliff, WOMADelaide, Adelaide, 2013

CAJUN & ZYDECO

Keith Frank, Rock 'n' Bowl, New Orleans, 2007

Rosie Ledet, New Orleans Jazz and Heritage Festival, 2002

Rosie Ledet,
reproduced from New Orleans
Jazz and Heritage Festival 2000
program due to lost transparency

As the history books tell us, Louisiana Cajuns are the descendants of the Acadians—17th-century French colonists who settled primarily in the eastern provinces of Canada. British colonists deported the Acadians in the middle of the 18th century, and many migrated directly to Louisiana, then a Spanish colony, while others were brought back to Louisiana from France by the Spanish to help populate the colony and provide a buffer against British colonists.

From these French-speaking origins two schools of music developed, Cajun and zydeco. Each developed with its own instrumentation and style, and each has its own geographic and cultural base in Louisiana. Increasingly, the boundaries are blurring within and between each form, but also within and between popular Louisianan and American music.

My understanding of both musical forms is that while they may have originally derived from French ballads, today they are fundamentally two forms of dance music. Cajun music is driven by an upbeat folk style that depends on a combination of vibrant fiddle and single-row accordion. Zydeco also relies on the accordion but the instrument is the old-world multi-row type, and the music is propelled by harder, deeper rhythms which are driven by electric bass and

the unique intensity of spoons on metal washboards.

Cajun is more conducive to a classical style of dance, whereas zydeco feels much more bluesy and funky. I guess it comes down to the difference between contemporary vestiges of European gentility adopted by the French Acadians as against the adaptations of black Creoles (descendants of French and Spanish colonists mixed with Native Americans, Haitians and Africans), who have added blues, R&B, soul, reggae and Afro-Caribbean music to the Cajun-influenced waltzes and shuffles.

BeauSolieil avec Michael Doucet is the most prominent exponent of Cajun music, although Doucet is no traditionalist. He is part of a contemporary school that pushes the boundaries of traditions to include blues, jazz, bluegrass and Louisiana swamp music.

If you visit Jazz Fest, watch out for the Cajun dancers—colorfully dressed with feathers in their hair, waltzing and two-stepping at the front and side of the Fais Do-Do stage which caters predominantly to Cajun and zydeco music. If you time it just right, you might just catch the watermelon dance—a choreographed group ritual that ends with a watermelon being

Buckwheat Zydeco, New Orleans Jazz and Heritage Festival, 2012

Keith Frank, New Orleans Jazz and Heritage Festival, 2009

Dwayne Dopsie, New Orleans Jazz and Heritage Festival, 2001

Nathan and the Zydeco Cha-Chas, El Sid O's Zydeco Club, Lafayette, 1998

Nathan and the Zydeco Cha-Chas,
El Sid O's Zydeco Club, Lafayette, 1998

split and shared among the throng. The Jazz Fest version, I am told, as colorful as it is, is tamer than at some other local festivals, where the leader of the ritual wears a tutu and brandishes a samurai sword to dissect the melon. For reasons that do not require an explanation, a samurai sword is not on the list of items that can be brought into Jazz Fest.

In 1998 I took a side trip from the Jazz Festival to visit Cajun country. Like any music form in southern America, and probably anywhere in the world, the weekends are the best time to catch the music as this is when the clubs and venues are open. Clubs and music venues in smaller towns, however busy on Friday and Saturday nights, are often either closed or very quiet midweek. My first stop was Friday night at El Sid O's in Lafayette, a zydeco club which features Nathan and the Zydeco Cha Chas; I think the club was owned by Nathan's brother. I was particularly struck by how comfortable the club felt and how languidly the dancers moved to the upbeat rhythms. I felt like I was some latter-day Robert Frank, taking photographs that included the American flag draped above the stage.

In my favorite image from this visit (see previous page, 213), I have deliberately manipulated the final print to reduce the club scene to black and white, but retain the color in the flags. The image, I think, works better in black and white, but the flags work better in color. The flexibility of digital imagery allows both to be achieved, without, I believe, compromising the image. When editing images for this book I uncovered another image from this visit, this time side stage, which I have pretty much left as originally photographed. I can't really explain why this one doesn't need the same manipulation—sometimes you make decisions about an image because it just feels right.

The following day I head to Eunice, the home of traditional Cajun music. First stop was the Liberty Theatre, a 1924 vaudeville/movie house now renovated and listed on the National Register of Historic Places. This is as old school as you can get, with music and dancing in the style of the Grand Ole Opry or Louisiana Hayride. The event is a live broadcast, in Cajun French language, of the Rendez-Vous des Cajuns radio show, and my presence is noted by the host. It seems they do not get much visiting media, and certainly not from Australia. I am interviewed on air during the show and think nothing of it until I arrive at my next stop, Fred's Lounge, in Mamou.

Fred's Lounge is an extraordinary scene that turns day into night. You enter into a darkened bar and it's as if you have stepped from the midday sunlight straight into a late-night bar and music venue. The drinks are flowing and the music rises above the chatter. There is a young accordion player—just a boy, obviously a prodigy—leading a band of old-timers in an upbeat waltz. I go to introduce myself, but they cut me off—they had heard me on the radio and were expecting me to arrive.

In a break in the music there is a rowdy competition for a prize of Cajun spices to the person who has travelled the furthest to be at Fred's on this day. I wait for the cities and countries to travel from the east of the USA and then across to Europe. A New Zealand couple enters the competition and they think they are taking the spices home. I scream out "Australia", and the spices are mine!

There were a few more stops on this trip, but the light was poor and I was much more interested in soaking up the atmosphere than taking photos, which would have required flash and a change in the mood (and my reception) at each venue. The Cajun dance hall I visited was very old-world and noticeably multi-generational. I have a very fond memory of being swept around the dance floor in a pale imitation of an elegant waltz.

The zydeco clubs were altogether different – much more like the juke joints of Mississippi. They were in ramshackle old buildings in poorer rural towns. The music did not start until very late, and the atmosphere had that edge that goes with any late-night drinking and dancing establishment.

The crowds were exclusively black. It was not threatening, and people were friendly and pleased I was there, but it was impossible for me to feel anything other than an outsider.

My last stop was a very late night Keith Frank concert. Cars and people filled the streets around the venue, which looked like a large old house with a very low ceiling. The wooden floorboards creaked with the strain of hundreds of young people dancing with abandon. The crowd reminded me of the kind of all-night dance party I might occasionally go to in East London—black, hip, young and there for the music. It was very dark, and this was the new generation of zydeco; Frank was mixing hip hop and R&B dance music with zydeco, and the crowd was moving as one. I left while the party was still jumping, happy in the knowledge that the future of zydeco is in very good hands.

Watermelon Dance, New Orleans Jazz and Heritage Festival, circa 1996

Fred's Lounge, Mamou, 1998   Charles Neville and Michael Doucet, New Orleans Jazz and Heritage Festival, 2014   Cajun dancing at the Fais Do-Do stage, New Orleans Jazz and Heritage Festival 2012

ROCK
& POP

Chuck Berry, New Orleans Jazz and Heritage Festival, circa 2000

In recent years, the Jazz Fest program has increasingly leant on high-profile marquee names to attract numbers. This is probably a sound commercial decision to ensure the festival continues to run at a profit. It ensures continuity of the festival and provides a substantial source of funds for a range of cultural support programs for the other fifty weeks of the year.

It is not without controversy: many locals resent the increase in prices and the focus shifting away from local artists and jazz luminaries. This resentment has spawned smaller alternative festivals, such as the hugely enjoyable Chaz Fest, which was established to cater to alienated local artists in the mid-week period between the two weekends of Jazz Fest.

I can make three personal observations regarding the rock programming at Jazz Fest. First, I am glad that the festival continues to promote local culture and continues to turn a profit to support the maintenance of that culture throughout the year. Second, I am pleased to note that the cross-fertilisation of some of the visiting big names and local artists continues, and that this is helping the next generation of New Orleans artists to reach larger audiences. And third, and for purely selfish reasons, I am pleased to have had the opportunity to see some big-name artists that I might otherwise not have seen.

In this regard, I hark back to a couple of Jazz Fest moments that stick in my mind from 2012. One of the downsides for photography with these big rock acts is that the photo pit is increasingly being closed down, so you can either struggle to get a position in the crowd or choose to work at one of the other stages. For Tom Petty in 2012, I chose the crowd option. I set myself up in the early part of the day and befriended a young couple who agreed to keep my spot for me while I went off to shoot at other stages.

Left: Brian Wilson, New Orleans Jazz and Heritage Festival, 2012

Below: Bruce Springsteen and John Fogerty, New Orleans Jazz and Heritage Festival, 2014

John Stamos joins the Beach Boys, New Orleans Jazz and Heritage Festival, 2012

I was happy with the resulting photographs, but what I gained more than anything was a valuable insight into the mass culture of a stadium-size rock concert. Firstly, I admired the stamina and resolve of fans to hold their position for many hours throughout the day in hot and humid conditions. And secondly, when the concert began, I gained a rare insight into the mass ritual of tribal adulation for a big rock act.

The crowd was jammed solid and each member seemed to know every word and every nuance of every song. This wasn't just enjoying the concert; it was a mass exercise in reliving personal moments and memories. At one point I was standing next to a woman—probably in her '40s—who wasn't just singing along, she was screaming along. If truth be told I wanted her to stop, so I could hear Tom Petty doing Tom Petty, not one of his fans screaming out of key. But that would be to miss the point: this is a concert format for each and every person in the audience to commit to in their own way. And that required two things—a shared adoration and celebration with over 100,000 others, and a personal outpouring of past and present

joys, losses, aspirations and heartaches triggered by familiar lyrics. I prefer the considered and listener-friendly cerebral/spiritual approach of a jazz concert, but for the vast majority of people it is clearly a different story, and this speaks volumes for the power and passion of popular music.

In the same year, but on a different evening, Bruce Springsteen was headlining on the main Acura stage, while Al Green was performing on the Congo Stage. If you walk between the stages on the infield of the racetrack, you walk past one of the food areas. At about the spot where you might be lining up for a Crawfish Monica—one of the most popular local dishes—you can hear both stages at the same time. In my right ear: Bruce Springsteen, probably the greatest living rock performer; in my left ear: Al Green, definitely the greatest living soul performer. As an emblem of those very special moments that only happen at Jazz Fest, and keep on happening year after year, this is as good as any.

Top, Left to Right:
Crosby, Stills and Nash, New Orleans Jazz and Heritage Festival, 2003
Elton John, New Orleans Jazz and Heritage Festival, 2015
Lenny Kravitz, New Orleans Jazz and Heritage Festival, 2000
Dave Mathews, New Orleans Jazz and Heritage Festival, 2009

Bottom, Left to Right:
Ed Sheeran, New Orleans Jazz and Heritage Festival, 2015; Keith Urban, New Orleans Jazz and Heritage Festival, 2015;
Robert Plant, New Orleans Jazz and Heritage Festival, 2008; Paul Simon, New Orleans Jazz and Heritage Festival, 2001;
Tom Petty, New Orleans Jazz and Heritage Festival, 2012; Little Richard, New Orleans Jazz and Heritage Festival, 1994;
Cyndi Lauper and Charlie Musselwhite, New Orleans Jazz and Heritage Festival, 2011

Rock & Pop - 221

AFTERWORD

FROM SILVER GELATIN TO PIXELS—SOME THOUGHTS ON PHOTOGRAPHY IN THE 20ᵀᴴ AND 21ˢᵀ CENTURIES

One intriguing reaction to my musings on the music industry from friends and colleagues has been an unexpected and unanticipated interest in the role of the photographer and the changing nature of photography. In my first draft of this book I had included, almost as an aside, some thoughts about the nature and technique of photographing musicians in the expectation that a small handful of technophiles or industry specialists might be interested. That just about everyone who read my first drafts commented about these throwaway lines genuinely surprised me. I put this down to a changing relationship with photography brought about by the digital age. In the 1980s, when I was learning the craft of film-based photography, the cost and processes involved with shooting and processing film or transparencies was much, much higher than in the digital age.

Today's point-and-shoot cameras are cheap and cost-effective. They provide both immediacy and uniformly high-quality images. Digital storage is cheap and reusable; and sharing of images need not require expensive post-production or hard copy prints. This digital revolution has dramatically changed photography, but not necessarily always for the better. Digital imagery rewards instant gratification and, in my view, promotes mediocrity as a universal aspiration. It does this because there is no longer any expectation or requirement for an image to endure beyond a few hours, whereas in the past, the express or implied role for photography was to provide an historical record for current and future generations. Digital imagery is predominantly disposable. It relegates striving for the decisive moment, or searching for the artistic or social/political statement, to the very margins of the photographic mainstream, when once it was a central and driving force.

How we look at images has dramatically changed. The intimacy of poring over transparencies on a light-box or rocking a developer tray to slowly reveal the positive image, which just seconds before was projected light (through a negative) on to a light-responsive resin or bromide paper, is now almost completely lost to our collective sensitivities. Instead, we mediate almost all our images through the digital prism of a computer screen or mobile device. Even those images which were originally created on film suffer the same fate: nearly everything we now see (including all the images in this book) has either been created digitally or scanned from the original to a digital form.

Digital media, however, is not without its attractions. The evolution of fine art digital printing has progressed so fast that the combination of the finest quality inkjet printers and papers now produce fine-art prints of archival standard. Manipulating a digital image in post-production is almost infinitely flexible, and extremely accurate. Once saved, a manipulated digital image is much more likely to produce consistent editions of subsequent prints than trying to match successive prints in the darkroom. And the ability of modern-day digital cameras to take high-quality images in low light is breathtaking—particularly for anyone who has struggled to push a negative or positive film past 1000 or 1600ASA.

I have come to regard myself as one of the last generation of craft photographers. I wasn't quite up to mixing my own chemicals and making my own papers, but I did learn how the silver gelatin process worked and I was dedicated to extracting the highest quality from the materials and processes I had available. I have consequently spent many years breathing photographic chemicals in the red twilight of the darkroom, a muted and enclosed workplace that creates its own sense of time and space. As a consequence, the inevitable move to digital processing came, for me, as something of a relief. It's not that I didn't enjoy the darkroom process—there is always something magical about an image appearing before you as you gently agitate the developer tray—it's just that the smell and inhalation of chemicals was something I was happy to leave behind as belonging to a previous era.

The life of a photojournalist back in the days of black and white film required long hours in the darkroom inhaling chemicals. I recall rarely being happier in my photographic career than the day I installed an extractor fan and light-proof vent in what by then must have been my seventh or eighth darkroom in London. I would shoot portraits and stories by day and concerts by night. I would then manually process the film using a purpose-designed formula of chemicals, time and agitation to suit the sensitivity of the film stock and the light source in which the photographs were taken.

That first moment when the film was fixed and the negatives could be viewed was always revelatory; you simply couldn't relax until you knew you had captured the image. And then, even with years of experience examining the reverse tones and composition of 35mm black and white negatives, the nagging uncertainty about the final image could never be assuaged until the negative had been placed in the enlarger, paper exposed, processed through the obligatory three chemical trays (developer, stop, fix) and then examined under normal light.

And the process didn't stop there. Next stage was adjusting the exposure (by time and/or enlarger lens aperture) while 'dodging' those areas (small and large) that were too dark at standard exposure. This involved intercepting the light between the negative and the exposed paper for varying degrees of time depending on the desired effect. Many photographers use their hands for this task, but I preferred waving a hand-made tool: a doubled-over piece of gaffer tape, cut to an oval shape about the size of a small fingernail, and attached to the end of an unfolded paper clip. This cheap, replaceable and adjustable apparatus would manage both confined and larger areas of the image depending on the shape and size of the tool and how close to the light source it would be held.

Then followed 'burning'—the practice of adding light to selected areas of the print—to add tone to highlights and darken mid-tones or shadows. For this task, I used a piece of flexible cardboard, usually about 10 x 12 inches in size, with a small hole cut in it. Light would pass through the hole (which could vary in size and shape as needed) and be directed to the areas requiring additional light. I would invariably use a second sheet of cardboard, without a hole cut in it, to 'burn' each edge of the print so there would be a graduated tone (from dark to light) from the outer edges of the print. This was intended to stop the eye wandering away from the image by bringing the focus of the gaze towards the primary subject.

Once processed through the obligatory three trays of chemicals, the normal light could be turned on to check the quality of the image. At this point, you might start over, to correct or adjust one or other parts of the process; or perhaps use a cotton bud dipped in potassium ferricyanide to manually lighten shadows or bring out some specific mid-range or highlight detail, particularly in skin tones; then fix again and wash thoroughly in running water.

This process might take a few short minutes or many longer minutes—time being an elastic concept in a darkroom. On the one hand, the precision of the exposure to light is measured in units of seconds. On the other hand, the time ensconced within the darkroom could be measured in lost hours of uncertain duration. For example, I could spend all night working on one exhibition print. The 'dodging' and 'burning' could take anywhere up to ten or fifteen minutes per print, and the processing time on fibre-based prints was always extended to allow the full range of tones to come in over a minimum 120-second period in the developer tray. The slightest possibility for improvement would warrant another print, and then another, and so on.

Many a morning I would wake up after a six to eight-hour marathon session to examine up to twenty prints drying on my living room floor. Invariably I found it hard to tell which print was the final print; the minor gradation and nuances I had so fastidiously attempted to tweak the previous evening were not so clear in the light of the day. Or, I would wake up to realise the overnight drying of the print had revealed I had not achieved what I thought I had in the early hours of the morning: some areas of the print or key details were too dark (either over-exposed or under-'dodged') or too light (under-exposed or not 'burned' enough). And so the process would start over, until it was just right.

When the print was dry, there was always one final step: 'spotting'. This refers to the practice of using a paintbrush and ink to disguise small spots or fine hair lines on the final print. This comes about because, even with the most careful cleaning, it is impossible to avoid tiny specks of dust settling on either the negative or the enlarger lens. As the light is projected through the negative, this dust interrupts the light passing through to the light-sensitive photographic paper and shows up as a white spot or mark on the processed print. This may not be a problem when the mark is on a white part of the print, but it is very noticeable against any shade of tone.

My spotting technique is a little different from those of others, who dilute the ink to achieve a matching tone of grey. I dry a small quantity of ink by swirling it around the inside of a white plastic container (cream cheese or yoghurt containers always worked best). This creates a range of grey tones dried to the inside wall and floor of the container. I then use a moistened paint brush (very fine tip) to choose the correct ink tone and remedy the print—the secret is to start light and build up to darker tones. It is always time-consuming and painstaking, but very satisfying when a spot or mark or scratch completely disappears.

Thinking back on this period of late-night printing sessions, I realise modern jazz was my all-pervasive soundtrack. My cassettes (for this was the pre-CD era) would invariably be the peaceful meandering of Keith Jarrett (the Koln and Bremen concerts were favorites) or some early Jan Garbarek or other ECM label recording of the time. These contemplative but melodic musical pieces complemented the timelessness and soft intensity of uninterrupted darkroom sessions in the pursuit of unachievable excellence.

There was never a shortage of film to process or prints to make. It was a badge of honor (or calling card) for professional photographers to shoot one day and have a selection of prints on the desk of the commissioning editor the following morning. Timeliness and consistent quality is what distinguishes professional photographers from amateurs and wannabe pros.

In my experience, picture editors do not expect an award-winning image from every commission, much as we all would like to achieve this. What they do require is a high-quality image that will fulfill the requirement to illustrate a portrait or story or live review.

and composition, which distinguishes one photograph from another. An amateur might be fortunate enough to have better light or more interesting elements within the composition for the fraction of a second he or she is recording. But the amateur lacks the pressure of the obligation to get it right every time. For an amateur, it is disappointing if an image fails. For a professional, however, an image that doesn't work can damage your career. Perhaps professionals should be judged not so much by our best images but by how consistently we perform, particularly when circumstances aren't ideal.

I remember a talk I gave during my short residency at the Victoria and Albert Museum in London in 1989, at which I explained that photographers needed to be prolific because the only way to get to the result you were chasing was to shoot a lot of film. I explained that while people might be impressed with a handful of images I could show them, they may have been less impressed with the thirty or more images rejected for each one selected. On a similar note, I remember a shoot for the *Observer* magazine on bullying in schools. One student asked me why I was taking so many photos. I answered very honestly, "because I make so many mistakes." I am not sure he believed me.

Back in 1989, there was genuine interest in the nature of the art form and how photographers might approach what it was they were trying to achieve or communicate. In my case I made it clear that I thought photographers had an obligation to use their art and skills to make a contribution to social change. However, unlike today, there was very little interest in the mechanics of photography or the perspective of the professional photographer as a practitioner.

My love of photography originated in my perception of its ability to communicate information and human emotion. I was enchanted by the idea that the medium could change the way people think—about subjects they were familiar with, and about subjects they were not but should understand better. The decisive moment captured by Henri Cartier-Bresson and Elliot Erwitt were early influences, but it was the social realism of early American photojournalism that resonated with me most. The extraordinary dustbowl photos of the 1930s by the likes of Dorothea Lange and Walker Evans, and the pioneering work of Margaret Bourke-White and Robert Frank were major influences in my approach to photojournalism.

Black and white images, for me, have the power to define the essence of a situation or reveal a concealed emotion in ways that color photography cannot. It requires sensitivity to light and tone, but above all, it requires the photographer to consider and understand the content of the image. Colour photography always seemed to me much more about form and shape than emotion or content. And in the early years of my career, black and white photography met the needs of newspapers and magazines: there was no requirement or expectation that colour photographs would be preferred.

Whatever the light conditions, whatever the subject, or however many obstacles are put in your path, it is the photographer's job to provide a selection of images that fulfil the brief. The last thing you or a picture editor want is to end up without a useable image.

It is this ability to provide a high-quality, useable image even when the obstacles are profound—for example, poor light, an uncooperative subject or unreasonable time pressures—that distinguishes amateurs from professionals. When the conditions are ideal, there is often very little to separate them, and many times an amateur can end up taking a better photograph than a professional. An amateur might understand the content and context more completely, or might, by luck or skill, choose a better fraction of a second to freeze and preserve than a professional.

It is worth remembering that every exposure is usually about 1/60th or 1/125th of a second or thereabouts; only in very rare circumstances does a photograph capture more than a

My empathetic approach to photojournalism—built on my youthful work promoting land rights for Aboriginal Australians—was based on trying to reflect the subject's point of view and being as non-interruptive as possible; notwithstanding the whole relationship was artificially mediated by the presence of a camera. While I may have had some early success in reducing the distance between the photographer and subject, particularly in my west and east London projects, I have increasingly become more and more uncomfortable with the role of the photojournalist and the impact he or she has on the people and environment in which he or she is working. In this day and age of universal media-savvy, it is almost impossible for the photographer to 'disappear', or at least fade into the background. The pretence of 'recording' or 'documenting' is questionable when the presence of the camera invariably or inevitably changes the dynamics or relationships in any situation.

This is probably one of the reasons I have come to focus on music photography almost exclusively—because I do not have to change or impact upon the relationship between the artist and the audience in order to take photographs. By and large, it is an accepted part of the industry that musicians need photographers. Our role in studio or location publicity shots is premeditated, collaborative and usually contractual. Our role at concerts should not (and normally does not) change the nature of the interaction between the artist and the audience; what we are recording (almost always) is the artist's performance and interaction with the audience, not their interaction with the camera.

What I have found helps me most as a music photographer is to have a personal relationship with the music. My best photos are nearly always of artists I admire, even if on some occasions I have overshot in my zealousness to do a favorite artist justice. There is something about being in tune with the artist and the music, and wanting to represent that as faithfully and respectfully as possible, that improves the photographic process. It helps me to know, or feel my way into where to stand, which angle works best and which moment to capture. It makes me work harder to get a better picture, because I want the image to endure for all those who were not as fortunate as I to be present at the gig.

In my obituary of David Redfern, I applaud his ability to achieve a quality of timelessness in his live music photography by reference to a photograph of Buddy Rich featured in the award-winning feature film *Whiplash*:

That image, about as close to perfection as a live image of a jazz drummer can be, was taken side stage at Ronnie Scott's jazz club in London in 1969. …The small fraction of a second it took to squeeze the shutter came about as the confluence of a number of factors. Redfern had access because he had earned the confidence, respect and friendship of both Ronnie Scott and Buddy Rich. He knew where he needed to stand (seemingly close enough to the horn section to be rubbing shoulders with the trombone player); he had the eye, and patience, to frame the image dramatically; he had the sensitivity to know (and feel) when

the moment was just right; … and he had the craft and skill to ensure his exposure was exactly right.

The resulting print effortlessly sings. Some 45 years later, a young film director has recognized Redfern's achievement in this photograph: he has placed the viewer as a participant in that singularly intense moment of artistic creation. … He invites those of us who were not present to feel as if we were, or to imagine what it would have been like to be there; as if Buddy Rich is playing for us, right now, and forever. Could there be any greater accolade for a concert photograph?

Redfern manages to achieve this quality timelessness again and again with his live music photography. His joy of music is not limited to stylish representation. He wants the viewer to cherish the artist's performance as much as he does. He understands that one of his pictures, one of those squeezes of the shutter, might be ascribed the role of summing up a musician's lifelong pursuit of musical excellence.

Neville Brothers, House of Blues, New Orleans, 1994

This description of Redfern's work may help to explain why some of my proudest images are those that are used to illustrate obituaries. This may sound morbid, but music photographers are very aware (or in my view, should be aware) that their images may one day be used to sum up a person's artistic life. Knowing how important an obituary image can be for family and fans focuses your mind on producing an image that may have the power to do justice to the life and the person you are photographing. This is indeed the antithesis of disposable digital imagery, because the purpose is expressly to create an enduring image for all time.

The best example I have of an image photographed with an obituary in mind is the image of Cab Calloway looking up (heavenward?) towards the spotlight above him. The most poignant performances I can remember are Herbie Mann performing with an oxygen mask in the jazz tent at the 2003 Jazz Fest and Johnny Adams performing in the Jazz Fest gospel tent in 1998 with Aaron Neville, fully aware that he had only a few months to live.

I remember discussing this part of our work with the former stage manager at the jazz stage in New Orleans. He told me there is a look, a 'death mask', he could see on artists he had known for many years. It was clear to him that they had just a short time to live, and he would consequently ensure photographers had good access to record what might be one of the artist's last gigs. This stage manager had a unique way of balancing the needs of the audience and the role of the photographer. Many photographers at the front of the jazz stage did impact on the audience, but some of the most important artists in the world were giving memorable performances that needed to be recorded. The solution: a restriction of time or songs at the beginning of the concert, and then reopening access for the end of the concert or the encore; everyone went home happy.

I often find myself the lone photographer in the photo pit dancing, clapping along, or hollering for an encore. I do want to take great pictures, but I also want to enjoy the concert. This normally goes hand in hand; although I am prone, as I think most music photographers are, to retrospectively filter my enjoyment of a gig in direct proportion to the quality of the images: a great performance with mediocre images is unlikely to rate as high as a mediocre performance that produced great photographs.

I simply can't understand why some photographers cultivate an attitude of indifference to the performance. Usually the artist doesn't notice the photo pit, but sometimes they do, and I like to think they prefer seeing someone enjoying the show than looking bored or distracted. I do not have time or interest for those photographers who radiate a stylised machismo in their desire to get 'the shot'. They remind me of the worst excesses of the Fleet Street packs or the paparazzi. They exemplify why I feel estranged from the world of contemporary photojournalism, because I cannot abide by being motivated almost exclusively by 'sales', rather than by creative or artistic or ethical intent.

There is an ongoing tension between aspiring to great art and trying to earn a living. Sometimes the two aspirations coincide, but often not. When I finally came to move more towards shooting in color—probably about the early to mid '90s—it was the commercial imperative that pushed me in this direction. I was always interested in applying the art of photography to capturing the essence of the performance, but what sold, as the sales personnel at the Redferns library kept reminding me, was color. The tighter, sharper and brighter the image, the better.

In retrospect, this may have been the beginnings of a wider regressive movement towards dumbing down photography. Not surprisingly, commercial motives were at work. If it didn't sell, and it didn't get published, then what value did an image have other than personal indulgence?

It is very hard to hold on to the future historical value of the photographic record when images are languishing unseen. I remember, for example, an image I took of about five young horn players at the Café Brazil in New Orleans; I think it was in 1995. It was more of a midweek rehearsal than a concert—there may have been just two or three others in the audience—and none of the young men was a big name at the time. The library could see no reason to archive and caption the image, but I regret not insisting on its historical importance, as the image has not survived. Each of those young men has gone on to become band leaders in their own right, and the authenticity of this early collaborative work would have told an important story.

It is also very frustrating to find that magazines and picture editors always seem to pick the weakest image for publication. Sometimes it is very hard to believe that the picture choice is anything other than wilfully mischievous. I guess it is possible that picture editors know and understand their audience better than a photographer does, or perhaps they 'read' the images without the context of the photographer's knowledge of the event or his or her artistic intent; but just sometimes it would be rewarding if our best images were the ones that were used. Safe to say, the images chosen in this book are primarily my choice, and so I guess a book edited by someone else, might look altogether different. Another intriguing observation is the way an image tends to gain value and recognition proportional to the size or prominence of the reproduction. A full page or cover image is received very differently from a stamp-sized

Joe Strummer (The Clash), Brixton Ace, London, circa 1982

reproduction, even if the smaller image is superior by any objective criteria.

As my career has progressed I have moved through a variety of equipment that started with the basic OM1 Olympus SLR camera (with which some of my best images were taken) and then graduated through to Leica M and R cameras and lenses (German rangefinder and SLR cameras and lenses with the highest technical quality, and prices to match); and ultimately to Nikon SLR cameras and lenses (a year or two after autofocus was first introduced and other professionals started extolling the virtues of this new system).

The year I decided to test digital photography—by hiring a digital SLR back for my Nikon lenses—changed my relationship with photography forever. I had anticipated, back in April 2003, that I would shoot a handful of images in digital, but stick to my normal count of around ten–twelve rolls of film at each day of the New Orleans Jazz and Heritage Festival. By 2003, my tenth Jazz Fest, I had already begun to restrict my black and white photography to a handful of more prominent or historically significant artists. There was simply no commercial demand for black and white images, and contemporary processes could easily convert a color image to black and white if needed.

The first ten or twenty frames on that digital camera changed everything. Seeing the images on the camera back—almost instantly—caused me to abandon film photography. Gone was the previous uncertainty associated with delivering the film to the lab the following morning, and then returning the next day to see whether I had caught the right moments and at the right exposure. For the first time in over twenty years I could know whether or not I had captured what I had intended, as I shot it. I could correct exposures and I could re-shoot if the image wasn't quite right. I could also relax and enjoy the gig if I was happy I had captured the image or images I needed. A good example is my Robert Cray picture from 2009; my fourth or fifth frame was as good an image as I was ever going to take of this artist. I put my cameras down and had the rare privilege of enjoying the rest of the gig.

In those early years of digital photography, we were much more innocent of the hours of post-production that would be expected and required to edit, manipulate and upload images, and still to this day I prefer to get the exposures and composition right, thereby avoiding as far as possible the need for digital manipulation. This may also be because I was always obsessive about exposure and framing. My photojournalism was almost always printed full negative, including the black line of the negative frame. I deliberately composed my images as full-frame and discouraged (but could not always prevent) cropping by over-zealous picture editors and graphic designers. With color transparencies, there was so little tolerance for exposure errors that you just had to get it right.

I had a shooting routine for each and every frame that started with a spot meter exposure reading on the face of the subject before every press of the shutter. This was intense and taxing work. It required a point-and-shoot action (I used a Minolta spot meter) to get an exposure reading. This was followed by a quick mental calculation of the correct exposure, adjustment to the exposure as needed (either by adjusting the shutter speed or lens aperture), then frame and focus, then shoot.

Prior to the introduction of lenses with automatic focus, intense concentration was required to find and hold focus, particularly with moving subjects. Think about repeating this as many as five or six hundred times a day and you can begin to understand why digital photography with autofocus felt like a liberation. Most of the hard work was gone, and you knew exactly what you had shot by looking at the back of the camera. This was not just the case for professional photographers. It was the case for all photography, and as the technology keeps improving it gets harder and harder to take a bad photograph. Fortunately, for people like me, it doesn't seem to have guaranteed a good or exceptional photograph every time. But it has made everyone who owns a camera capable of taking a good photograph and capable of considering themselves a photographer of sorts. This is not a bad thing—I am not decrying the demystification or democratisation of the craft, but it has changed the way everyone thinks about photography.

Nowadays, much of the interest in what I have to say about photography tends to come from people who enjoy taking photographs, and are curious as to what makes my (or any other professional's) photographs different, or special, or in a class that makes them stand out. But as the years go by, there are more and more photographers (or would-be photographers), taking more and more photographs, with seemingly fewer and fewer outlets to which to sell them. Where do all those photographs end up?

I have been asking this question for the better part of thirty years, and the volume of images being taken is increasing, not decreasing. I sometimes find myself in a photography pit with thirty or more photographers. Only a few are on assignment, and the remainder seem to be shooting for the same agencies, particularly now that the two majors have effectively monopolised agency distribution by purchasing most of the smaller

Herbie Mann, New Orleans Jazz and Heritage Festival, 2003

agencies. There is not a music photographer of comparable age or experience who does not bitterly complain about the way the industry now treats photographers, and there is a not a young photographer who doesn't struggle with the same issues—even if he or she has become accustomed to this kind of treatment as 'normal'.

I would not like to be a photographer starting my career today, and I want now to presume to articulate what I understand to be a collective frustration at what music photographers have seen happen to our industry and our professional lives. I think it starts with respect and understanding, or more importantly the lack of it. When I began my career, photographers were valued contributors to the industry. Artists and promoters would positively encourage photography—and go out of their way to help us gain access—because they knew that our images being published in magazines and newspapers was the lifeblood of the industry. Artists and their management, festivals and their promoters, all understood and appreciated the value of a strong image being published in a magazine or newspaper. The fact that we also earned an income from this process was welcomed, not derided. This was understood and accepted as mutually supportive. Never once can I remember this being questioned as exploitative. The relationship was symbiotic. It was mutually beneficial and warranted mutual respect. It was never about greed or ownership or appropriateness (whatever that means); it was always about shared artistic and commercial endeavor. Everyone was in it together. Everyone benefited.

Contemporary managers and promoters would, in my opinion, do well to recognize that facilitating the role of the photographer—by providing access, good lighting, and strong or graphic backdrops to shoot against—will enhance the likelihood of images being published, and the prominence the images are given. Similarly, artists would do well to follow the lead of artists like Walter 'Wolfman' Washington, Irma Thomas or Fats Domino, who always wear colorful and stylish clothing. This helps make the image 'pop' and makes it much more likely it will be published or published more prominently. On behalf of all music photographers in the world, a plea to all artists: please, please avoid white! If you want to know what works best, just ask us—any photographer worth his or her salt will be happy to assist.

One of the first questions people ask me nowadays is whether I had permission to take my photographs. This is a question that would not have been asked twenty years ago, because by and large the only people with cameras at a gig that were capable of taking commercially exploitable images in that era were working photographers. Usually we had access arranged in advance and were welcomed as professionals contributing to the industry. On rare occasions, we might be joined by an enthusiastic amateur. It was rare for there to be more than one or two photographers at smaller gigs and more than a handful at more important gigs. By and large we behaved ourselves and audiences saw us as just another part of the gig. We were part of the crowd, staking our claim to a good vantage point to enjoy the gig along with the other concert-goers. Many a time I would make friends or contacts with kindred spirits hanging out at front of stage waiting for a gig to commence.

It is also true that audiences behave differently depending on the nature and location of the gig. A rock or punk gig is often just a battle to secure a place at front of stage and to keep your footing while the crowd is moving. I memorably managed to keep upright on a chair—the lone chair in the concert hall—that I had commandeered at the side and front of the stage at a Clash gig in Brixton in London in the early '80s.

A jazz or singer/songwriter audience is normally comfortable with photographers, unless we do something to interfere with their enjoyment. Unfortunately, there seems to be a new breed of photographer—mostly larger males—who are unaware of their physical presence and the impacts on those around them. They do a disservice to themselves, other photographers, the artist and the audience.

An English audience is also totally different to an American audience. The first time I shot in New Orleans (in 1994), I remember trying to get to the front of stage for the Neville Brothers at the House of Blues. I lowered my shoulder and began to push my way through whatever gap I could find, just as I would at a London gig of comparable size. This seemed to unsettle the people I was attempting to move past; one asked me what I was doing and I explained I needed to get to the front of the stage. "Just say excuse me," I was told. I tried this out and to my amazement it was like Moses parting the Red Sea—a path was made and through to the front I walked with nothing more than an occasional "excuse me" and an apology. God bless America!

Nowadays, there is an increasing number of photographers with professional gear at every gig, and the quality of the hardware makes it more likely that each person with a halfway decent SLR and an autofocus long lens will take an acceptable representation of a live image. There is also a sizeable portion of an audience likely to have a point-and-shoot camera or a mobile phone that is capable of generating an image of acceptable quality for potential commercial use or uploading on one of the many platforms now available on the internet. I welcome this democratisation of image taking, although I don't quite understand the contemporary need to prioritise the digital sharing of an experience over the personal appreciation or participation in that same experience. What I absolutely do not welcome is that this new photographic paradigm should be extrapolated to cast a restrictive net over working photographers.

The movement towards restricting photographers to the first song or first three songs of a concert, is now almost universal. I find this both perplexing and frustrating. It started in earnest, as I best recall, in the early years of this century, and has now become commonplace. While I can understand some circumstances where it may be warranted—for example, to avoid interfering with the enjoyment of the audience—there are many concerts where this simply does not apply. How do we affect the audience's enjoyment when we are out of view either in a photo pit or side stage? How is it that film or video cameras—which are usually much less discreet—do not attract the same opprobrium? While I can also understand that artists may not want flashes going off throughout a gig, the simple solution is to prohibit flash photography. I have never liked flashes being used at concerts and contemporary digital cameras now perform very well in very low light.

In my experience, artists and their audiences universally want to see, and enjoy, quality images of an artist in performance. And they want to see and read about artists and concerts in their physical or digital magazines and blogs. So why restrict photography to the first song, or the first three songs? The view that a photographer should be able to shoot all that is needed in the space of one or three songs is a bit like saying that an artist should be able to lay down the final recording in the first take. Sometimes this works, but not always, and no one would or should mandate this every time. Who can possibly predict that the single and precious moment of photographic interest in a concert will occur in the first one, two or three songs? From my experience, this is very rarely the case—the artist is far more likely to be warming up in the early part of the show, and it is the middle and latter parts of a gig that tend to elicit the profound emotional and physical moments that translate into a unique and memorable still image.

Neville Brothers, House of Blues, New Orleans, 1994

What do these restrictions mean for working music photographers? It means we aspire for little more than a sharply focused, correctly exposed and tightly composed image of the artist or artists doing whatever he or she does. We are largely reduced to technicians with less and less opportunity for art or interpretation. Is it any surprise that our art and our craft is dumbed down and disrespected? We simply do not have the time to feel our way into the mood of the gig, or work our way through capturing an image that is special or remarkable. In the frantic few minutes we have, all of us are chasing a single useable image—usually of a single performance cliché.

In short, we are all chasing the same image at the same time, and fundamentally we are all going to get the same or similar images, or minor variations on the same theme. No wonder we are treated as expendable! Essentially then, it is a circular process. The restrictions on our access restrict our originality, our approach and our art. This restricts the esteem and reputation with which we are treated. This makes it perfectly acceptable to restrict access because nothing of what we are doing is original.

A colleague and jazz critic shares my disdain for this artificial and arbitrary restriction on concert photography. He poses the question—why critics aren't similarly restricted to the first one or three songs? It is unthinkable and foolish to think that a critic can write about a gig having missed most of it. But the same consideration does not apply to photographers.

It's even more outrageously frustrating when we can see large numbers of the crowd snapping away with mobile phones; at most larger gigs now it is getting harder and harder to control image-taking with mobile devices. So is it that the artists and their management prefer the distribution of substandard images on mobile devices to high-quality images by professionals?

The artificial restrictions are getting more and more onerous. Artists and their management are now issuing contracts that are intended to restrict our ability to on-sell images. The worst I have seen (so far) came in the form of an email on 7 June 2013 from the very helpful publicity agent responsible for managing photography at the Melbourne International Jazz Festival. The email asked if I would accept the following photography policy being imposed by Cassandra Wilson's management:

1. Ms. Wilson must receive hi-res exact duplicates of all shots immediately following the shoot.

2. Ms. Wilson must approve all photos to be used for publicity, promo, etc.

3. Ms. Wilson has the rights to use all photos for any purpose in perpetuity.

The notion that Cassandra Wilson (or her management) would presume to demand all rights for any purpose in perpetuity is by far the most draconian requirement I have come across in the industry. I wonder what Cassandra or her management would say if I asked for all rights, in perpetuity, to her music?

All this means I find it very hard to recommend photography as a career to any young person today. Even without the overlay of unprecedented job losses—the result of massive restructuring as the print media industry responds to the digital future—the role and status of the photographer has become increasingly marginal.

Maintaining independence in this environment has also become very difficult, if not impossible. For many years I and other like-minded photographers have resisted giving up our copyright to publications or agencies. However, there is more and more pressure to relinquish our rights with minimal recompense. As the jobs market contracts, the individual photographer's bargaining power declines. As major agencies swallow smaller agencies and libraries, there is less room in the market for independent photographers. Getty Images, for example, have now bought the two specialist libraries I worked with in the UK. Getty Images will prioritise access for a staff photographer over a contributor (presumably because a contributor gets a percentage of the royalties, whereas a staff photographer does not).

I have no problem if images by another photographer sell ahead of mine—that is, and always has been, the nature of the industry. If another photographer gets better images than mine, I am happy for him or her, but annoyed at myself for not achieving a similar standard. In my view, the best or most suitable images will be rewarded because they will be chosen by the paying client. An essential problem with the way the industry is evolving is that the client's choice of images is being restricted. The circle closes yet tighter.

About the only upside I can see is the slowly growing recognition of music photographers and photography in museums and art galleries. Perhaps if this trend continues, the pendulum can swing back to something much closer to mutual respect.

Trumpet Black leads the New Birth Brass Band celebrating the life of Kirwan James, New Orleans Jazz and Heritage Festival, 2015

Photograph courtesy of Michael Weintrob - www.michaelweintrob.com

Australian-born Leon Morris is a multi-award winning photojournalist. He has dedicated over 30 years to exploring his passion for the roots of contemporary music.

From 1982 to 1994, he worked in London, building a high profile photography career that saw him regularly published in prestigious publications from *The Guardian* and the *Observer* to *Time Out* and *Face* magazines. He won a number of major photography awards, was appointed the Victoria and Albert Museum's first photographer-in-residence and was profiled on BBC Television as one of Britain's leading young exponents of photojournalism.

In 1994, increasingly disillusioned with the direction of the media industry, he returned to north Australia to work with Indigenous Australians in event production and public policy. He now lives with his family in Melbourne and works at La Trobe University. He returns to New Orleans each year to add new images to his extensive archive.